YOUR GUIDE
TO GOOD SHELTER

YOUR GUIDE
TO GOOD SHELTER

How to Plan,
Build,
or Convert
for Energy Conservation

Carmen and Brownlee Waschek
Photography by Carmen Waschek

Reston Publishing Company, Inc.
A Prentice-Hall Company
Reston, Virginia

Library of Congress Cataloging in Publication Data

Waschek, Carmen.
  Your guide to good shelter.

  Includes index.
  1. House construction. 2. Dwellings—
Energy conservation. I. Waschek, Brownlee,
joint author. II. Title.
TH4811.W348   690′.8   77-22275
ISBN 0-87909-963-1

© 1978 by Reston Publishing Company, Inc.
A Prentice-Hall Company
Reston, Virginia 22090

10   9   8   7   6   5   4   3   2   1

Printed in the United States of America

To our son,
    Matej Albin

CONTENTS

PREFACE

The home you might have built in bygone days is no longer possible. Inflation's impact is staggering and the need to conserve energy is imperative. Your dream home, the home you've wanted so long, must undergo a metamorphosis in order to become a reality. You will be compelled to consider new ideas in design, materials, and equipment; some luxury items may have to be postponed because of cost or energy consumption. Some changes will be subtle and others bold—but your home can still become a reality if you evaluate your needs carefully and plan realistically.

In spite of all the problems attendant to building *now,* the planning and final realization of your home should be an exciting, wonderful adventure. Living in it should be a happy, pleasant experience, fulfilling all your hopes and desires and rewarding your sacrifices and efforts.

YOUR GUIDE TO GOOD SHELTER is a practical guide to help you plan and build your home, or convert certain elements to save money and energy. It contains sound, proven information, not idle theories. Energy conservation measures discussed in Chapter 8 were designed into our home—and they work! "Chinquapin" uses 46 percent less energy than other homes its size in the same climate. Cost-cutting measures discussed throughout the book cut Chinquapin's price in half, but retained the total concept and feeling of the first plan.

This volume deals not only with cost and energy conservation, but with the human aspects of building and living in a home. It is not written as an architectural textbook filled with detailed technicalities over which you ultimately have no control. It is a realistic book, written in language you understand, and dealing with situations you will encounter. It is written from experience. We, too, are homeowners, and our home is an integral part of our lives. As such, we give you a new perspective into building, deliberating at length on planning your home to meet your family's needs and touching on the fragile area of human relationships which can erode away the whole project if not skillfully handled.

A well designed architectural edifice should be structurally sound, functional, and aesthetic. But when that edifice is also a home, we must add two more qualities: it should be livable and affordable. YOUR GUIDE TO GOOD SHELTER will help you achieve all these qualities.

ACKNOWLEDGMENTS

Special appreciation is given designer W. D. Farmer and builder George Bramlett, Jr., who transformed our ideas and theories into the reality of our energy-efficient, economical, and livable home. W. D. Farmer, Inc. is further acknowledged for contributing all house plans and drawings in this book.

We would also like to express our gratitude to Georgia Power Company for energy studies in Chapter 10 and for the opportunity to investigate and photograph that company's experimental Solar Energy House in Atlanta.

Invaluable energy research facts were contributed by the Atlanta Gas Light Company, to whom we are grateful.

And to all builders, suppliers, workmen, and others who contributed their time and expertise, and opened their businesses and homes to our prodding questions and cameras, we thank you—American Olean Tiles of Georgia, Inc.; Dr. and Mrs. Clyde Anderson; Winford Baker; Charity and Rob Berling; C. David Bishop, Jr. and family; Mr. and Mrs. Bill W. Blackstone; E. B. Burney; Cary Bynum; Lonnie H. Cato; Jimmy Q. Childress; Cofer Bros. Inc., Building Supply; James O. Conner; Craig's Camera House; Decatur Federal Savings and Loan Association; Daniel Lee Dixon; Mr. and Mrs. J. Robert Douglas, Jr., W. J. Fortenberry, President, F. E. Fortenberry and Sons, Inc.; Phillip A. Gibson, Southern Solar Systems, Inc.; B. J. and Margaret Goble; GreyBear Enterprises, Inc.; Mr. and Mrs. Robert Hash; Jake Hilton; Mr. and Mrs. Richard Human; Jerry Johnson; Jimmy Wells Builder, Inc.; Fred S. Kerr; Bro. Leo Francis; Mr. and Mrs. Walter P.

McCurdy, Jr.; Fr. William McGuirt; Marion McLean; Dave Menna; Max F. Munoz; National Association of Home Builders; Northside Contractors, Inc.; Judy and Bruce Olderman; Dick and Sara Anne Pepper; J. C. Penney Co., Perimeter Mall, Atlanta; Fr. Bob Pierce; Mary Theresa Poole; William R. Probst, President, Smoke Rise Corp.; Progressive Lighting, Inc.; Russ Reed; Southeastern Plumbing Supply Co., Inc.; Skillern and Morton, Inc.; Dr. and Mrs. Charles R. Stearns; Kathy Stearns; James W. Stephens, Sun Ray Labs, Inc.; Joseph N. Wagner; E. Reynolds Wheeler and family; Paul G. Winder.

INTRODUCTION

There's no point in building if you can't have what you want.

So, what do you want?

The answer is more than just a number of bedrooms and baths. A house is a collection of rooms, but a home is more—it is a unity of ideas, thoughts, purposes, and people. It is a oneness where house and family work together for your goals. Your home is *you*.

Your home will be your refuge from the tensions of the world—your place of safety and security where you can rest and refresh yourself. Man is like an animal returning to his den to lick his wounds of battle and to rest. Man, too, must have a place to go, and it should be home.

A new home is a fresh start, an improvement, a symbol of achievement. It will give you identity. It will be your place to entertain friends and carry on family activities. Your home reflects *you* and projects your image, and you will want it to be beautiful, inspiring, and stimulating. It will be your family's environment and the place where your children's memories are made. It's what they will come home to.

What do you want in a home? Simply, a dwelling that meets the needs of your family. What are those needs? You must identify them—all of them. Because *only after you have identified your needs can you begin to plan a home that meets them* and is, therefore, what you really want. We would be foolish to say that all your needs can be met—that you can have everything you want—because the offerings are endless and their costs constantly spiral upward. Nevertheless, the total concept and feeling you desire can be yours if you identify your needs and plan carefully for them.

Each family member should have some area of his own—it gives a feeling of security and belonging. Men especially are neglected in this way: their bedrooms usually are feminine, their dens have become the family room, and their workshops have been taken over by Mom's découpage. Don't slight the children either. They need a place to play both inside and outside. If you don't provide it at home, they will find it elsewhere, either in the street or at the neighbors'. Finally, don't forget Mom—give her a corner somewhere that she doesn't have to share with anyone.

While identifying and analyzing your needs, remember that full enjoyment of your home can be achieved only if you are financially at peace with the world. If your mortgage is so big that you dine by candlelight out of necessity and partake of beans and sardines the last ten days of the month, then you're on the brink of financial disaster. Scale down your desires so you can afford to enjoy your dream home.

Think long and deeply about your needs. Then as you develop your plans, your home, whether cottage or castle, will acquire an intangible quality that communicates to every passerby that it cradles and protects its family—that it is a part of their lives.

YOUR GUIDE
TO GOOD SHELTER

PART 1

PLANNING

Select your lot in fall or winter when the contour of the land is revealed. Only then can you see problems that may be hidden by lush summer foliage.

1

VOCABULARY

Much of the language of the building industry has specialized meanings not found in standard dictionaries. Familiarize yourself with the following building terms so that you can communicate successfully with people in the industry.

ABOVE GRADE   Above the surface of the ground.

APPRAISED VALUE   The potential market value as determined by a professional appraiser.

AWNING WINDOW   A window that is hinged at the top and that opens by being pushed outward at the bottom.

BACK-FILL   To fill the excavation around the foundation.

BACKHOE   A machine used to dig trenches.

BACKSPLASH   The wall area adjacent to and back of a counter top.

BATT   A factory prepared unit of insulating material (usually fiber glass with paper on one side). It is stapled into the areas between studs and joists.

BATTER BOARDS   Rough boards erected at the corners of the house site in the beginning stages to accurately locate perimeter walls, corners, and floor levels.

BELOW GRADE   Below the surface of the ground.

BOARD FOOT   A cubic unit of measure for lumber, equal to a board 1 foot square by 1 inch thick.

BTU   (British thermal unit)   Unit of heat measurement. One BTU is the amount of energy required to raise one pound of water one degree Fahrenheit.

BUCK   The contents of the scoop on a front-end loader; a scoopfull.

BUILDER'S PRICE RANGE   The usual price local builders pay for materials in their standard houses. A small selection of samples falling into this narrow price range often is set aside in building supply showrooms for customers who buy ready-built houses still under construction and who thus can make their own selections.

BUILDING LINE   A line that shows how close to the street building is permitted.

BUILT-IN OVEN   An oven separated from cooking elements and built into the cabinetry at any desired height.

BUILT-IN RANGE (SLIDE-IN)   A stove with its own base, designed to fit between cabinets.

BUILT-UP ROOF   A roof built up in place using several layers of felt covered with tar and gravel. A built-up roof can be used only on flat or slightly sloped surfaces.

CASEMENT WINDOW   A window that opens as though it were hinged at the side.

CAULKING   Soft, rubbery material used to plug small cracks where materials join—especially around outside doors and windows.

CLEARING   Removal of trees, shrubs, undergrowth, surface rock, and debris at the building site.

CLOSING   The signing of all final papers concerning building, buying, and mortgaging. The house should be finished and all parties mutually satisfied at this time.

CLOSING COSTS   The cost of doing business with the lender, including items such as his attorney's fees, appraisal, transfer taxes, recording fees, and your credit investigation. Closing costs may range from 3 percent to 6½ percent of your loan and sometimes can be included in the total amount borrowed.

CONSTRUCTION LOAN   A short-term loan made to finance the building of a house. After the term expires, the loan is replaced with a permanent mortgage loan. Some lending institutions make combination construction and permanent loans, collecting closing costs only once, and charging interest only as the money is used during the construction loan term.

CRAWL SPACE   Space under the house or in the attic large enough for a person to get in to work on pipes, wires, and so on.

CREDIT INVESTIGATION   A search to determine an individual's credit worthiness.

DEAD BOLT   A heavy, elongated metal bar forming part of a security lock. It extends into both door and door facing.

DOUBLE GLAZING   Two layers of glass *not* hermetically sealed as in insulating glass. One layer is removable. There is no perceptible difference in the insulating qualities of sealed and unsealed layers, and their uses are similar. Double glazing is cheaper, whereas insulating glass is easier to clean.

DOUBLE-HUNG WINDOW   A window in which both the bottom and top halves move up and down.

DOUBLE JOIST   Two joists used instead of one to give extra stability and support.

DROP-IN RANGE   A stove made to "drop in place" in a series of cabinets. It does not have its own base but rests on a base constructed as a part of the cabinet system. Unseen portions of the stove's sides are usually unfinished.

DRYING-IN   Enclosing the house with water repellent materials in the early building stages to keep the interior dry.

DRY WALL   Sheetrock.

DUCTS   Large pipes.

EARNEST MONEY   A moderate sum of money placed by a potential buyer in the hands of the seller to show his "earnest" intention to buy. It will apply to the purchase price if the transaction is completed, but it can be forfeited if the deal falls through.

EASEMENT   A portion of land set aside for specific use with which the owner cannot interfere, such as drainage, sewer, or public utilities.

ELECTRONIC AIR CLEANER   (Electrostatic filter) A device that electronically attracts and removes particles from the air.

ELEVATION   Front, side, or rear view of a building. Its visual appearance.

ESCROW ACCOUNT   An account set up by the lender to accumulate that part of monthly house payments designated for taxes and insurance.

FASCIA   The covering over ends of the roof rafters at the edge of the roof overhang.

FILL DIRT   Dirt used to fill a hole.

FINISHING NAIL   A headless nail that can be driven deep into a finishing material. The resulting small hole can be plugged, leaving little evidence of the nail's presence.

FIXED GLASS   A window that does not open.

FLASHING   Sheet metal used as a waterproof barrier at the junction of two materials.

FLITCH   A thin piece of wood used as veneer in plywood paneling.

FLUE   A pipe used to carry off gases from a furnace, fireplace, or hot water heater.

FLUSH DOOR   A flat door without design.

FOOTAGE   The interior area of a house.

FOOTING   The supporting base of a house; it is always made wider than the walls it supports.

FRAMING   Construction of the skeleton or frame of the house.

FRONT-END LOADER   A machine of the bulldozer type with a loading scoop on the front.

GRADING   Reshaping the land.

GROUT   Fine cement-like material used in laying ceramic tile.

HEADER   A horizontal timber placed above a door or window opening to support the structure above it.

HEAT LOSS   The speed and amount of heat transmitted through a given material—its insulating ability. (The heat loss of an entire house should be computed to determine correct size furnace and air conditioning units.)

HOLLOW-CORE DOOR   A door made of plywood sheets over a rectangular wooden frame, leaving the interior center portion hollow.

HOPPER WINDOW   A window hinged at the bottom that opens by being pulled inward at the top.

HUMIDIFIER   A device that adds moisture to the air.

INFILTRATION   Air seeping into your home through cracks around windows, doors, and other structural openings.

INSULATING GLASS   Two layers of glass hermetically sealed with a layer of dry air between them. Insulating glass is used in windows and doors to reduce heat loss in homes with large expanses of glass or in homes located in extreme climates. The additional cost of insulating glass is quickly offset by savings in heating and air conditioning costs.

JALOUSIE WINDOW   A window made of several horizontal sections that open in a manner similar to a Venetian blind.

JOIST   A supporting timber set on edge in floor and ceiling construction.

KILOWATT HOUR (KWH)   A unit of electrical energy equal to 1,000 watt hours. A 100-watt bulb burning for ten hours will consume one kilowatt hour (KWH) of energy. Residential consumption of electricity is measured in kilowatt hours.

LAMINATED BEAM   Small timbers stacked and glued together to form a larger and stronger beam than can be obtained from a single, solid timber.

LAMP   Light bulb.

LIVING SPACE   The part of a house that is finished and heated.

LOCK   Any device to hold a door shut, including door knob sets as well as security locks.

LUMINOUS CEILING   A ceiling covered with fluorescent lamps behind plastic diffusion screens, giving the effect of a soft, even glow over the entire ceiling. This is especially effective in windowless areas, kitchens, and baths.

MASONRY NAIL   A nail that can be driven into masonry.

MOLDING   Decorative finishing trim used around doors, windows, ceilings, and floors.

MORTGAGE   An agreement in which money is borrowed, using real estate as security.

MUD   Soft, clay-like material used in dry wall construction to cover seams and nail holes. It dries, hardens, and then may be sanded smooth.

MUNTINS   Small wood or metal strips that divide a window into panes.

ON CENTER   A term used in measuring the location of framing timbers. Such measurements go from the center of one timber to the center of the next, thus eliminating the thickness of timbers from all calculations.

PANELING   A sheet of wall covering manufactured in convenient sizes for both interior and exterior use. Paneling is made from a variety of materials including solid wood, plywood, and synthetic products.

PAPER HOLDER   Toilet tissue holder.

PERCOLATION TEST   A test to determine the suitability of soil for a private sewer system.

PIER   Masonry pillar used to help support the house.

PIN   An iron spike driven into the ground to mark property lines.

PLAT   A scaled map showing planned or existing divisions and developments in an area.

POST LANTERN   Outside light mounted on a post by a drive or walk.

POURED FLOOR   Finished floor made in place from liquid materials (concrete, terrazzo, plastic, etc.) poured and allowed to harden. Sometimes called *seamless floor*.

PRELIMINARY PLANS   The first set of plans used for estimates, bids, and revisions. Architects' plans are complete in every detail. Designers' custom plans are complete enough for accurate estimates and bids but may lack detailed drawings not needed at this time.

RANCH   A one-story house.

REAL ESTATE   Land and whatever is attached to it.

RECORDING FEE   The fee charged by a governmental unit for recording a real estate transaction in official records.

ROOF OVERHANG   The portion of a roof that extends beyond the house.

R-VALUE   Resistance to heat loss. A method of evaluating insulation, written as R- followed by a number. The higher the number, the greater the resistance to heat loss, and therefore the better the insulation. Doubling the R-value does not cut the heat loss in half.

SAFETY GLASS   Glass that will not splinter when broken.

SANITARY SEWER   A sewer that carries off household water waste.

SEALER   Material used on porous surfaces, such as wood or slate, to plug the pores and seal the surface to absorption.

SECURITY DEED   The document that passes title of the mortgaged real estate to the lender, as security for the loan.

SEPTIC TANK   The underground settling and decomposition tank of a private sewer system.

SHAKE ROOF   A roof made of rough wooden shingles.

SHIM   A small wedge used to level or straighten an object, such as a door or window frame.

SIDING   Originally, wooden boards used to cover exterior walls. Other materials are also used now.

SLAB FLOOR   A poured, solid concrete floor.

SLIDING WINDOW   A window in which the ventilating portions slide on a horizontal track.

SOFFIT   The finished underside of the roof overhang.

SOLID-CORE DOOR   A door without a hollow interior.

SPECIFICATIONS   Detailed descriptions of materials and equipment to be used in a house.

SPLIT   (Split level) A house with three levels—two stacked, with the third adjacent and midway between them.

SQUARE   A unit of measure equal to 100 square feet.

STACKING   Much paneling has vertical grooves to simulate the junction of boards. When paneling is to be pieced, as on a 10-foot high wall (most paneling is 8 feet high), the grooves must coincide precisely one over the other to appear as continuous boards. This is called *stacking*.

STAIRWELL   The area containing the stair.

STAKING   Marking on the land the future location of structures and related items.

STOOP   A small porch.

STORM SEWER   A sewer that carries off street drainage.

STUD   A timber used in constructing the skeletal portion of walls.

SUBCONTRACTOR   Specialized workman (plumber, electrician, cabinet maker, etc.) the builder hires to do a job requiring a specific skill.

SUBDIVISION   A planned neighborhood of dwellings usually located in suburbs.

SUBFLOOR   The first layer of flooring laid on the floor joists. It underlies the finished floor.

SURFACE UNIT   Stove-top cooking elements separated from the oven and used in conjunction with a built-in oven.

SURVEY   An accurate determination and marking of the boundaries of a piece of land. A survey map can also show structures and improvements. (All surveys should be made by professionals.)

THERM   A unit of heat equal to 100,000 BTUs. Natural gas is measured in therms.

TITLE   A document stating ownership.

TITLE SEARCH   A search of official records to determine ownership and unearthed claims of indebtedness on a piece of real estate.

TOPO   Common term for topographical survey.

TOPOGRAPHICAL SURVEY   (Topo) A contour map showing the rise and fall of the surface of land in addition to boundaries, trees, streams, and other outstanding natural features.

TRACTOR   This term refers to both the small bulldozer used in clearing and the farm-type tractor used in landscaping.

TRANSFER TAX   Tax charged by a governmental unit when real estate changes hands.

UNDER ROOF   The stage of a house after the initial roof has been built.

VENTILATING GLASS   The part of a window that opens.

V-GROOVE   A deep V-shaped groove cut into paneling to simulate the junction of boards.

WARRANTY DEED   A document that transfers ownership of real estate.

WATER CLOSET   Toilet, commode.

WEATHER STRIPPING   Strips of metal, rubber, felt, or other materials used around doors to stop drafts from coming through.

WINDOW LIGHT   Window pane.

2

SELECTING AND BUYING YOUR LOT

"LOTS FOR SALE—SALESMAN AT FIELD OFFICE" the sign reads. When you have house-building fever, your heart skips a beat at this sign and you can't resist a look at the lots. The friendly salesman on duty gladly tells you all the great things planned for the area and explains the good deal you get during the "special introductory price period." "Look! There's a perfect lot with a beautiful shade tree and a little stream at the back. Just what I've always wanted!" you exclaim. "Quick, buy it now before the price goes up!" your impulses urge. "Buy before someone else gets it!"

Stop! Don't sign that paper! Take the brochures, look around, and go home. You have some serious homework to do before you select your lot.

When you embark on this exciting adventure, there are many aspects you should consider about every potential lot. So if you have your heart set on the one with the beautiful tree and the little stream, put on the brakes long enough to give it a good, hard look based on the following points, because careful selection of the correct lot is essential to the realization of your total desires in your new home.

City or Country?

Are you tired of the rat race and pollution of the city? Do you want to get away where you can hear the birds and wind in the trees? If you do, then look for land in the country, but before you go out and try to buy the lower 40 from Farmer Brown for a song, remember there are many prices to pay for the peace and solitude you seek. First, Farmer Brown has been to town and knows what his land is worth—especially to you!

What about its location? Will you still work in the city? If so, how will you get there? Is public transportation available, or will you have to consume costly gasoline driving back and forth? How much time are you willing to spend commuting, and what about convenience to schools, shopping centers, hospitals, and doctors? What services, social life, and cultural opportunities are offered by the quaint little village nearby? Would it provide diversions during the long winter months; and where could you pick up your favorite Chablis? What about police protection, and would the village fire department come if needed, and to what could it attach its hoses? How much would your insurance rates be? Is there a paved road to the property, or would you have to build one? At what cost? (Sometimes the expense of building a road can exceed the cost of the lot.) How many vehicles would you have to maintain now and when the children are teenagers? Could the gasoline consumption be justified?

Another aspect to consider is whether you actually could get your home built in the country. An artist designed a beautiful, but simple, home to be built outside the small town where he worked and then found that no local builder would touch it because it was "so different." The "so different" feature was an exterior of wood siding instead of the usual brick. To get men who would work on his home the owner had to import them at extra expense from a distant city.

Could your village supply men and materials for your house? If not, could you find workmen and suppliers willing and able to travel from another city? If you want the simple life of the early pioneers, fine. But if you like modern American conveniences, activities, and services offered by the city, then think again before buying, building, and moving to the country.

Subdivisions

Lots found in suburban subdivisions may offer the best of two worlds—city and country. Reputable developers buy large tracts of land, divide it into lots, pave streets, build drainage systems, install sewers, lay water mains, and bring in other utilities. The projects are planned for their accessibility to those things most families want—schools, shopping centers, medical facilities, and highway networks. Some are served by public transportation systems, an important factor for gasoline-conscious buyers. Better developers, sensitive to the environment as well as the dollar, capitalize on the natural beauty of an area, disturbing little and preserving natural vistas as much as possible. Living in such a community can provide nearly everything the country recluse might want and at the same time give easy access to all the benefits of urban living.

Neighborhood

The total neighborhood is the most important factor in determining the appraised value of your home and its resale price. When you buy a lot, you buy not only that plot of earth on which you will build your home but also part interest in the entire neighborhood within sight and extending for a radius of a mile or more. So when you look at land, don't be blind to unkept yards down the street or heavy construction going on a mile down the road. Those areas are part of your neighborhood too, and although resale price may not concern you now, the evaluation of your neighborhood will be a major factor in securing a mortgage to finance your home. (Identical houses on quarter-acre lots can vary 100 percent in value because of the neighborhood.)

If you're a gambler at heart, seek your new neighborhood in the newest development where you have the pick of the area, with a plenitude of lots from which to choose. You can select the biggest and best of the entire offering and have a real advantage over the hundreds of other lot seekers who may come later, but those latecomers will carry with them the secret of what the neighborhood will become. When first buyers view the area obstructed by nothing but the wonders of nature, it's impossible to predict what future neighbors' personal tastes and habits will be, even if costs and restrictions of the area make it possible to predict their incomes. Even prestige neighborhoods can deteriorate if the residents don't keep up the property.

As you stand in the midst of a primeval forest surveying the developer's brochures, remember there is a chance involved. Future neighbors could be incompatible. They might build houses you would not enjoy looking at daily, or future inflation could cause a reduction in lot size and house quality, lowering the whole level of the neighborhood. Your house would be termed "overbuilt" and would be worth very little more than the average of the others regardless of its size, quality, or cost.

If you want to avoid this gamble, select an established neighborhood that you like. Examine it carefully, observe each home, and try to determine the type of people who own them. Are the yards well kept? Have the houses been repainted recently? Where do the children play—in the street, the neighbors' yards, or have the parents provided areas within their own yards? Here you know who your neighbors would be and what their modes of living are. You already know what you would see out your windows and from your patio. But price is proportional to desirability, and you must expect to pay more for land in a nicer, established neighborhood with fewer chances of deterioration.

The last lot in an established neighborhood is not without risks; it has its own special kind. Namely, why hasn't it sold already? Is there something wrong with it that everyone but you knows? Play detective and find out. It may flood with every rain, or not have a clear title, or perhaps it was too hilly, too wooded, and too rocky for other lookers, whereas its "faults" could provide the perfect union between house and land for you.

When your home is finished and you have moved and settled, what relationship do you want with your neighbors? Do you wish to get together for cookouts several times a week, or do you prefer individuality where each family is a separate, unique unit, having few close relationships within the community? Ascertain the general personality of a prospective neighborhood and whether you would be happy living in the midst of the established style. An older couple might find close proximity to swinging, jet setters a bit too much for their constitutions, and the latter might die of boredom if they build an exciting modern home in a neighborhood where the major sport is shuffleboard and all political discussions center around the Truman administration.

Will you be compatible with the neighbors? Do you have similar feelings concerning major issues, and is your life style harmonious with the customs and expectations of the community? If you desire no close relationships, then mere acceptance of you is adequate, but if you wish to develop warm and lasting friendships with an exchange of ideas, there must be some similarities in beliefs, goals, heritage, and culture. You must have some things in common other than income to nourish and develop a happy rapport. Supercharged feelings concerning religion, race, or any other emotional issues can make compatible relations impossible.

Zoning

It's a shock to build your dream home—putting in a year or two of backbreaking yard work perfecting your landscape—and then find the daisies and wild geraniums you have enjoyed in the meadow next door replaced by a sea of used cars. It can happen if there's no zoning, or existing zoning is lax and easily changed! Falling into such a trap may be avoided by examining at the local courthouse or borough hall the most recent zoning map of your prospective lot and its surrounding land. Although it may appear to be safe, land can be rezoned to allow industry, apartments, and shopping centers in once exclusively residential areas. What are the trends in the general area? Does industry appear to be moving closer and closer? Are there undeveloped tracts of land that could be sold and rezoned? Is the area marginal or transitional? Is spot zoning allowed, and who are local authorities more sensitive to—homeowners or big business? Some situations are beyond the property owner's ability to anticipate or control, but many zoning problems can be foreseen if the prospective buyer will investigate before buying his lot and building.

Costs

If cost is no concern, the only financial interest you have is the resale value of your property, and perhaps not even that. But if you must consider cost and have a ceiling that you cannot exceed, then you have many financial concerns. First, don't invite disappointment by selecting a lot in an area that you can't afford. You might buy the lot and never be able to build a home on it because you find that building costs and restrictions governing the minimum house size in that subdivision are higher than you expected. If you managed to get the house built, could you afford to furnish it in the style you desire and then maintain it? A two-acre lawn is beautiful if properly cared for, but who would care for yours? Could you afford a yardman, if such a luxury was to be found, or would you have to do your own yard work? Do you have time for that or would you have to "moonlight" to make house payments? *You must know your limitations and be realistic, not emotional.* Nothing is more pathetic than a formal garden starving for fertilizer and water because the owner can't afford these necessities after paying for the plants. Know your means and select a lot in a price range you can manage.

Consider also a very real, hidden expense: TAXES. Have the local tax office estimate the tax bill on your planned home on a particular lot. This can be a jolting realization! Experience the shock before you buy your lot and build—not after it is too late. Remember, however, that a high tax area usually gives you more services and security, whereas low taxes may be no bargain at all. You might find that a lot with low taxes is located in an area with no fire department, inadequate roads, poor building codes, no zoning, rationed water in the summer, and overloaded sewers.

Terrain

Some lots definitely are not suited for building certain styles of homes, and if you know the general style of house you wish to build, mentally place it on any lot in question and see how it fits. There should be a close aesthetic tie between house and land achieved by fitting the shape of the house to the contour of the land. Is the land sloped, and does your home require a flat lot? If so, you would have to alter the natural terrain, and that could destroy the entire character of the land. Likewise, forcing a multilevel hillside house on a flat lot also requires extensive alteration, which could create an artificial mountain and disturb natural drainage slopes, causing you and the neighbors endless problems. If, however, you place prime value on the land and intend to leave it in its present natural state, design a home to fit the terrain of your dream lot, whatever its contour may be.

Does the land have built-in problems to erecting any house, such as a stream that must be bridged before the first piece of equipment can reach the building site, or an excessively steep drop? Such problems can be solved with the aid of a professional planner, an extraordinary builder, and plenty of extra money. So as you shop for your lot, evaluate each lot's terrain and try to anticipate any problems it might present.

Size

How much land do you need for your home and outside activities? With less gasoline available for recreational purposes, you will be spending more of your leisure hours at home. If you plan to have a pool, tennis court, or rose garden to replace the weekend excursions you once took, remember the space they will require.

Selecting the proper size lot is one area of planning often overlooked by prospective owners. Failure to have enough land to do the things your family likes to do will create frustrations at home. Likewise, insufficient area in which to display a house properly can completely negate a striking exterior design. Estimate the space you need to display your home and for family activities. Lot size should be considered carefully, because it cannot be altered or expanded later as a house can.

Landscaping

You don't have to plan the details of landscaping at this point in your venture, but you should have in mind the general type you prefer. Observe the terrain to see if it offers the basic foundation for what you want. If you wish to have formal gardens and manicured lawns, seek level uninterrupted land. Or if you are an amateur naturalist who wants to live among ferns and wild flowers, your quest is for a wooded lot free of noxious growth. Does the lot have problems that might require more time and money to correct than you wish to expend? Erosion can demand endless work and expense to bring it under control before any pleasant landscaping can commence. Are there piles of decaying trees and trash that were dumped there when adjacent lots were developed? Estimate how much initial work will have to be done before you can enjoy your landscaping.

Soil

They couldn't flush their toilets! "They" were a number of families who bought beautiful, large lots in an exclusive new development, built their custom designed homes, and moved in. They were just settling down to enjoy the luxuries of pollution-free air, good fresh water pumped from their own backyard wells, and the peace and quiet of life in the country when the decision of the State Board of Health arrived: the soil had failed the percolation test. They couldn't flush their toilets!

How could such a ridiculous situation be true? The development where this unbelievable plight occurred was located several miles beyond the limits of the public sewer lines, and therefore each home had to install its own private sewer system (septic system). Such a system, initially designed and constructed as part of the house, adds little to the total cost. It performs adequately and efficiently—*if* the soil passes the percolation test. But the official test was made *after* the homes were completed, and it showed the soil to be of such a nature that it could not adequately absorb the discharge from the septic systems. Therefore, official approval was denied for the area. They couldn't flush their toilets!

Be sure that the soil of your prospective lot can support a septic system if there is no public line to which you may connect. Results of percolation tests are usually registered with local or state health departments. If no test has been run, a surveying or civil engineering firm can do the job for you at a reasonable cost.

Natural Forces

If you could examine your lot at every season of the year before you buy, you would realize that you are buying four distinctly different lots. Each season would reveal features hidden by the previous one. You'd never know that it was a paradise of ladyslippers and trilliums until you saw them in early spring, nor could you imagine the array of red and yellow leaves of the maples and aspens unless you saw them in

October. But because it's impractical to view a lot throughout the year before buying, the best time to select a home site is late fall. When the leaves are gone and the ground is bare, you see the true shape of the land, and you hear the sounds of the area better—trains, traffic, children, dogs, and winter warblers.

Regardless of when you select your lot, consider the seasonal elements of weather and climate because they greatly affect the energy consumed in heating and cooling your home. From which direction does the wind come? How severe is it, and are there natural breakers? How much sun would reach your house in summer and winter? How would the snow bank, and could you go in and out your drive?

Water

Primroses and trout lilies would be beautiful planted in the fern bank of that lazy little stream; but before calling the garden shop to order them, check with local civil authorities and see a map showing flood plains in the area. You would assume that if the lot is in a flood zone it would not be for sale. Check on that! It might be an area designated a "100-year zone" (it floods once every 100 years), and if it flooded last year, it may be safe to build on. But think twice if the salesman tells you that there's no danger, there has been no high water in *nearly 100 years!*

What is the maximum water level after a heavy rain? In addition to its normal volume, does the stream bed carry water from the subdivision streets—do storm sewers empty into it? Is there undeveloped land upstream that might contain other communities in the future, adding more drain-off to your stream? What's hanging high in the branches above? Trash and tin cans six feet above the water level indicate that at one time water reached that height. The area may not be officially classified a flood zone, but if *your* land is six feet under water, as far as you're concerned, that's a flood!

Today the idyllic little sylvan stream where you might quench your thirst or take a refreshing dip hardly exists. Is the stream polluted? Observe the plant and animal life it contains. What's growing on the banks? Absence of both plants and animals or the abnormal presence of algae should warn you to be suspicious of the purity of the water.

Are there bogs or springs that would restrict the foundation and basement of your home? If you are looking at beach property, is the shore line stable, or does it have a history of constant change, eroding right out from under houses and washing them out to sea?

Water on your property can be beautiful and fun if it is where you want it, when you want it, and in the amount you want. Present, but not under your control, it can be a worrisome, annoying problem.

Utilities and Services

An inquiry at the local courthouse or city hall can answer your questions relating to tax-supported services, and the salesman can enumerate those offered by the development company. Nevertheless, be cautious if he says they are *planned* rather than existing. Determine if the following utilities and services are available to any lot you consider.

UTILITIES

1. Are electrical power lines in?

2. Are telephone lines in?

3. If natural gas is used in your general area, is it available to this lot?

4. Where will the water come from? Is there sufficient pressure? Will you be able to sprinkle your lawn in summer, or is water rationed?

5. Is there a public sanitary sewer system?

6. Are the streets paved? Curbs? Sidewalks?

7. Have storm sewers been installed? Where do they empty? (Check this thoroughly because water from half a mile away might empty in *your* backyard.)

8. Does the cost of the lot include *full* utility development costs, or will there be additional utility charges?

GOVERNMENTAL SERVICES

1. Is there regular garbage and trash pickup? Curbside or backyard? How often? Is it efficient and reliable?

2. What about police protection? Is the area patrolled regularly? Do police come promptly when called? How high is the crime rate?

3. Which fire department would serve *your home,* and how far away is it? Fire departments are not all alike—some are efficient and successful, and others are not. Zoning might require that you be served by a different one than your neighbor (and your fire insurance rates vary accordingly). Is there a fire hydrant close by?

The friendly salesman would like for you to sign on the dotted line there at the site. Don't be rushed. This transaction is far more important to you than to the salesman. It is your future home; it's only a paycheck to him.

Engage an attorney to make a title search and draw up a sales contract. Money you spend for his fee will be the best spent in your life. While your attorney is at work, have a professional land surveyor make a new survey—resetting any corner pins lost to earlier bulldozers and placing wooden stakes at enough points so you can clearly see your boundaries. Get a certified record of the survey. If you need to finance your lot, discuss this with your lender (Chapter 16).

When your attorney and lender assure you that all legal and financial matters are in order, you are ready to sign the purchase contract in your attorney's presence.

You have bought your lot!

3

WHAT'S YOUR LIFESTYLE GOING TO BE?

Energy conservation will cause many modifications in your lifestyle, so take advantage of the fresh opportunity offered by a new home and neighborhood to make other long desired alterations in your mode of living. Make the new home fit you, rather than you adapting to it. So as you plan, don't think about what your life style is, but rather, what it's *going to be,* and plan accordingly.

Did Aunt Frances give you her Chippendale chairs as a wedding gift? And have you since bought things to go with them until now everything you own is of that period, even though you never particularly liked it? And, of course, the new house will be Colonial also, because after all, all your things are. STOP! Don't let sentiment and Aunt Frances's chairs cause you to live in eighteenth-century America the rest of your life when you really long for chrome and glass and wet-look vinyl.

"But we have so much invested in period furniture already, we couldn't afford to change," you say. You are right. It is expensive and troublesome to change styles, but make the change. You will find that the pleasure of being surrounded at last by things you consider truly beautiful is well worth it.

Plan your home to fit your anticipated lifestyle. Take your activities one by one and consider the following aspects of each:

1.   *What things are involved?* Furniture, objects, machines, instruments? Where will these things be kept when not in use? Will they be needed for any other activity? Will that change the location of the storage space?

2.   *Who is involved?* Who in the family? Who outside the family? Where will they sit or stand?

3.   *How much space is needed?* Can it be used for other activities? Which ones? How much storage space is needed? Will it be built-in or in units of furniture? Is the space justified?

4.   *Which room is usually involved?* Will that room be in the new home? Will it need any special accommodations?

5.   *How much energy is consumed?* How can that amount be reduced? Is the energy consumption justified?

The following activities are common to most families. You will have more to add because every family is unique.

Eating

Where do Americans eat? It was the kitchen in the early settler's house, when the stew pot went from fireplace to table. Sophistication came, along with affluence, and the dining room became the place. Every home had one and it was used daily. Then casualness entered the scene, and the dining room was deserted. Meals were served in the family room—passed through from the kitchen—and at that same time we also began to dine on the patio with mosquitos and smoke. Now we're back in the kitchen again, as we grab a quick bite on the run.

Where will you eat? Your quick meals—breakfast, lunch, snacks? Your leisurely meals—supper, Sunday dinner? Your cookout meals—weiner roasts, hamburger fries? Your formal meals—holidays, special occasions? How often will you eat out?

Grooming and Dressing

Four teenagers and two adults getting ready at the same time to go out for the evening is a more interesting performance than the attraction any of the six might be planning to attend. Add the dimension of only one bathroom, and you really have a circus. There was a time when only females spent long hours in front of mirrors—but not now. Males have found that they, too, can be attractive, and most of them exercise the privilege—young and old alike. But look at what has happened to the beautifying areas. It was chaos when only the "girls" spent hours bathing, dressing, and primping, but now with the men doing it too, there has to be more room for the whole operation, and storage space for all the equipment.

Walls and floors must endure a great deal of punishment. Clouds of hair spray that miss the head find their way to the entire area around the mirror. Do you color your hair? Nothing can be quite so permanent, or quite so difficult to cover, as hair coloring stains on a painted bathroom wall. Can everyone find the proper garments? What if someone is going swimming, hunting, or to the opera? Where will you store special occasion costumes?

Careful consideration should be given to your present and anticipated grooming and dressing needs (when the children become teenagers and their styles and interests change). Wisely chosen materials and correctly designed size and location of these areas can head off that dressing time confusion.

Laundry—Mending—Sewing

You may have a maid and seamstress to maintain your family's clothing, or family members may do it themselves. Either way, these activities require specialized, built-in accommodations such as plumbing, heavy-duty wiring, and exhaust vents that should be planned in advance. Efficiency and convenience are key words here, regardless of whose job it is to perform these activities.

Entertaining

We wore our evening clothes and the hostess fed us in the packing shed! It was supposed to be *the social event* of the year to christen their new luxury home in the plushest section of the citrus belt. Over 3,000 square feet of air conditioned comfort, and yet not a single room large enough to hold more than two extra couples—and she had asked a hundred! That was her usual style of entertaining, so why didn't she plan for it? We gasped for breath as the hot, steamy Florida night air pushed down around us. We made trite conversation as we tried to ignore beads of perspiration running down one another's faces. Mosquitos flitted around the light bulbs and fell into our warm champagne, while sand fleas chewed our ankles. What an evening to remember— when we planed our home! Ninety-five thousand dollars and still no place but the packing shed to have a party. Why, that's madness!

Your style of entertaining is as individual as your personality. It's one of the most prominent facets of your lifestyle, the one friends see most clearly and usually remember longest. Plan your total entertaining facilities so your guests will not be conscious of the backstage inner workings of the affair but will remember each occasion as a gracious and enjoyable event.

If your lifestyle includes evenings of music, plan a special area to accommodate musicians and audience. Because carpets and draperies absorb sound, avoid placing them in the music room.

What kind of parties will you give? Your professional, social, and civic commitments will influence this. Will you have intimate little dinners for prospective junior executives, cookouts for the office staff, buffets for Rotary, cocktails before the games, fondue after the concerts, bridge luncheons, coffees, teas, receptions, luaus, barbecues, or pool parties? How many guests will you want to entertain at one time? Will you seat them? Where? Will they be comfortable? Will your drive and street accommodate the cars? Do you need more off-street parking space? What about lights for the drive and walkways? Will guests flow easily from one party area to another inside the house? Where will you hang their coats, and can they reach a bathroom without passing through a private area? Where will your guests eat? Will you need a bar? Can your flooring take the spills and footwear? How can you facilitate cleanup afterward?

Every party has food. How will you prepare and store yours?

Even if you have a caterer, there must be adequate kitchen facilities —warming ovens, counter space, electrical outlets—for smooth service. If you plan to prepare your own food, you must plan your cooking units, refrigerator and freezer space, food preparation area, wine closet, and pantry to be of sufficient sizes and types to serve your entertaining style.

Where will your party things stay when they aren't being used? Your rotisserie, tables, chairs, lanterns, linens, silver, crystal, chafing dishes, and fondue forks must be remembered in planning storage areas.

Occasionally people such as encyclopedia salesmen and clergymen will drop in without invitation. Where will you seat them to chat? Will it be the living room, or is that reserved as a museum while guests are received in the family room? Children have visitors too—sometimes every day to play and other times for very special events such as birthday parties. Can your home take care of all these occasions? Maybe you need to isolate some areas from childish enthusiasm. Spirited, exuberant play is an excellent way for children to express themselves, but it may wreck Dad's concentration on the speech he is to make before the Chamber of Commerce. Let your anticipated lifestyle determine your home planning and design.

House Guests

Ten percent of your building cost can be tied up in the guest room. In the average home this room occupies 10 percent of the total footage, and it may not be used more than three or four nights of the year, or 1 percent of the time. With such little use the guest room becomes a far more extravagant luxury than a swimming pool, which may get 30 percent usage and cost much less than 10 percent of the house.

Some families have a constant flow of house guests, bringing entourages of pets and children, who enjoy the hospitality they receive and make their visit an annual occasion. For these families, a guest room is justifiable. Others live in close proximity to relatives (eliminating overnight visits) and find that business contacts usually prefer the privacy and freedom of motels to being "put up for the night" in a private home. Such families might find an innovative alternative to the standard guest room to solve their occasional house guest needs without tying up space permanently out of reach of the family's daily activities.

Education

Education is a continuous process. The early years are devoted to structured classroom studies, and adult years are often supplemented with enrichment and graduate courses at nearby community colleges or universities. These learning activities require quiet, well-lighted areas for reading and study and may also need specialized facilities depending on the nature of the studies. Both children and adults need reading and study areas out of the normal flow of traffic, where books and materials may be left undisturbed until the next thinking session. The kitchen table is *not* acceptable!

Office

Tax time! Where did you file the W-2s, or the tax and interest statement from the mortgage company, or the mileage on the cars? Managing a home and family successfully is like running a business. There are books to keep, supplies and equipment to purchase, insurance, bills, taxes, interests, loans, and payments to keep track of. You're doing the work of a small business office, and it will be simpler and more efficient if you have an office area located conveniently for the persons performing this necessary, modern family task.

Music

Is your piano a piece of furniture or a musical instrument? If it's the former, then place it where you and your decorator decide it will be most striking; but if it's the latter, you have other things to consider as well. Its room should be large enough to accommodate the instrument (a grand piano occupies more space than a bed) and its music. Rugs, heavy draperies, and upholstered furniture are acoustically undesirable because they absorb and muffle the clear, live voice of the instrument. Consider also other instruments that might play in ensemble with your piano. And remember the seating of your audience.

Gardening

In spite of sophistication, man is closely tied to nature. He has a feeling for the soil that stirs in even the most adamant "ungardener" at new home time, when the sweet smell of freshly turned earth at the building site stimulates a desire to plant a seed and watch it grow. When you begin to garden, you'll need a safe storage area for garden chemicals and tools. Both become more hazardous each season and should be stored safely away from small children.

One of the nicest inexpensive luxuries you can add to your plans is a simple gardener's shower in the basement or garage. Potting and arrangement space, a garden window, or a greenhouse can help make your gardening productive and satisfying.

A small greenhouse provides hours of relaxation in a favorite hobby at all times of the year. It costs little compared to the pleasure it provides.

Club Work

Scrapbooks, committee reports, and other projects are all part of club work, whether it's Garden Club, Civitan, or Scouts. Few homes are designed to accommodate club paraphernalia, although most families are involved in these activities. To avoid a spillover of papers and projects into your kitchen, dining room, bedroom, and family room, plan an area in which to perform your club duties.

Servants

If you're affluent enough to afford servants and lucky enough to find them, then your plans must accommodate their needs too. "Live-ins" must have comfortable *private* suites—preferably with outside entrances. Day or weekly employees will enjoy the privacy of their own bathroom and a quiet sitting area for their morning and afternoon breaks.

Fun

Fun is important to your life and adds a dimension of emotional stability to your family. Because there is less fuel available to have fun away from home, you'll need to plan more area at home for leisure activities. You might want to reinstate the family room as your family's fun room; that was its original purpose when it came into existence a few decades ago. Or perhaps you could make the children's rooms large enough for indoor play and build a hobby room, dark room, or shop for adult leisure.

Whatever your lifestyle is going to be, carefully evaluate your needs for every hour of the day, every day of the year. Only after you have identified your real needs can you begin to provide for them in your plans and conceive a home that will be livable and workable for *you*.

4

BE INNOVATIVE

Problems no longer exist according to contemporary philosophy; instead, we now have "opportunities." At this point in your planning your "opportunities" may seem insurmountable because your list of needs is so long that nothing short of Buckingham Palace could possibly have enough room, and your budget doesn't quite equal that of the royal family. How, then, can you possibly solve your insurmountable building "opportunities"? Innovation is the answer.

Innovation is the art of creating contemporary solutions from nothing more than need and whatever is at hand. A remarkable example of innovation is the igloo, the dome-shaped dwelling of ice blocks the Eskimo builds in a matter of hours in the frozen north. Faced with need for shelter from the cold and relentless wind of the Pole, and with no standard building materials available, the innovative Eskimo creates a dwelling from what is at hand. Because your needs are not as stark as the Eskimo's, and your solutions not such matters of life and death, your innovations will be more exciting and fun to create.

Priority must be assigned to your needs in light of the reality that you won't be able to meet all of them. Obviously, you shouldn't fret over meeting a need that is trivial to your family's lifestyle while overlooking something of utmost importance. The importance given to each need will help keep your ideas in proper order as you think about what you want your home to be.

What are all those annoying, ugly features you have seen in other homes that made you silently swear, "We'll never have that in *our*

Fixed glass in a large projecting window permits an unusual amount of natural light to enter. The window nook also provides a delightful place to curl up with a good book.

house!'"? Maybe it's an elaborate open Spanish grill separating the commode from the bedroom, or a kitchen undivided from the dining area (exposing all the cooking mess to the dinner guests), or perhaps your pet peeve is the double fireplace—that beautiful, unusable architect's creation that belches smoke into both rooms every time a door is opened. Exclude your pet peeves from your plans to ensure total enjoyment of your new home.

Innovation starts with deciding on the atmosphere of your home. Do you want a feeling of freedom and spaciousness created by high ceilings, great expanses of glass, and few walls; or do you cherish the

You can create the atmosphere you desire for each room by controlling privacy, visual space, noise level, and decor. A quiet, reflective atmosphere is achieved in this private area by installing a large window, thick plush carpeting, and a soft monochromatic color scheme.

cozy, warm, cave feeling of small, dark rooms shuttered from the outside world? *Privacy, visual space, noise level, and decor are all components of the atmosphere of a home.* Changing one or more of these components creates a different atmosphere, and you may find it highly desirable to vary the feeling according to the purpose of the area. An invigorating, inspiring reception area will stimulate conversation among your guests, yet you may want a quiet, restful feeling in the sleeping areas.

After you've decided (1) what you want your house to be, (2) what you don't want it to be, and (3) the overall atmosphere you desire, you are ready for the last and most productive step in your innovative process—*brainstorming!* Close your mind to every structure you've ever seen. Forget style, because it's largely a function of external finishing materials and surface details. Disregard standard rooms. Tear away from the influence of what your friends have just built and what your parents always lived in. Think of the best way to enclose space and to divide it into areas to meet your individual needs. You may suddenly discover you have no use for a living room—that vestigial organ of home building

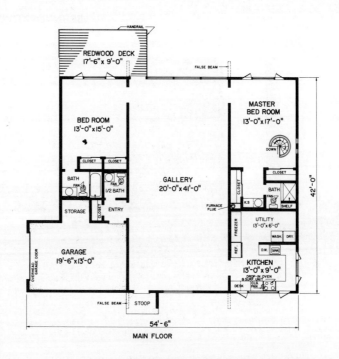

(a)

REDWOOD DECK
17'-6" x 9'-0"

HANDRAIL

FALSE BEAM

MASTER
BED ROOM
13'-0" x 17'-0"

BED ROOM
13'-0" x 15'-0"

DOWN

CLOSET   CLOSET

CLOSET

GALLERY
20'-0" x 41'-0"

42'-0"

BATH
FAN

1/2 BATH

BATH
FAN   SHELF

CLOSET

STORAGE

ENTRY

FURNACE
FLUE

K.S.

FREEZER

UTILITY
13'-0" x 6'-0"

WASH   DRY

GARAGE
19'-6" x 13'-0"

OVERHEAD GARAGE DOOR

REF

D.W.   SINK

KITCHEN
13'-0" x 9'-0"

DESK

DROP-IN OVEN
& SURF UNIT
CLG
FAN

FALSE BEAM

STOOP

54'-6"

MAIN FLOOR

(b)

Instead of the traditional living room, the authors designed a large gallery to serve their unique needs. (a) The room 20 feet by 41 feet with a 12-foot ceiling, has walls of glass at both ends to allow nature to enter. The spiral stair in the bedroom leads to the secluded library and studio below. (Courtesy of W. D. Farmer, Residence Designer, Inc.) (b) The authors' gallery ready for dinner and an evening of music.

32

—but instead, need an activity room combining the standard family room, living room, and dining room into one great room serving many purposes and creating a feeling of extravagant space. Through brainstorming you may arrive at an institutional bathroom with fixtures compartmentalized and lined up as the best solution for a large family. Your ideas may seem wild now, but that doesn't matter; you're in the innovative process through which you will create the best possible home for your family. Just remember, an igloo would never meet an Arab's needs any more than a tent would be suitable for an Eskimo.

ADD YOUR SIGNATURE

"Man Carving His Own Destiny," a massive sculpture of a primitive creature struggling to chisel his own form from a block of granite, stood in the courtyard of the home of its creator, Albin Polacek. This work spoke volumes about its sculptor, a Czech immigrant who struggled to carve his own destiny in America. Of all his noted works, it was significant that the artist had chosen this one to grace his own home, this one that was so autobiographical. This was his signature, and by adding it to a rather ordinary home, he made this home forever his in the memory of all who were privileged to visit it.

The same signature effect was created by a gentle lady who had no thoughts of art, but who was sensitive and sentimental and had collected over the years a horde of nameless memorabilia from excursions, events, and family affairs. She requested her designer to include a space for her treasures in her new home, and he designed a series of shelves, niches, and spotlights for her collection. There wasn't a piece of art in the lot (little of it was even attractive), and most of it was cheap tourist trinkets, but together it was a beautiful statement of an eventful life. It was her signature, and everyone who saw it felt the warmth of a real person living in that home.

Add your signature to your home by incorporating your family's treasures into your design. What are your treasures? Anything that is meaningful to you, evokes pleasant memories, or expresses your aesthetic tastes. You may have a beautiful collection of antique glass packed away in baskets in the cellar. If so, plan a sunny window with shelves to take full advantage of the sparkle and color of the old glass. A mounted deer head represents sport and fellowship to the man who bagged it, and it deserves a place of honor in his home because it's a part of his signature. It could be striking in the basement recreation room or in its own niche in the stairwell. Don't forget the rest of the family's sports accomplishments. Each plaque, medal, and trophy represents a challenge and victory and pleasant memories to the recipient. Shelves in an unexpected

The family coat of arms, handmade of stained glass and fitted into the family room wall, is lighted by natural light during the day. At night the coat of arms window is lighted by a well-placed spotlight. A sheet of plexiglass on the outside protects the window from breakage.

34

Designed and cast especially for this spot by a Trappist monk in a nearby monastery, this sculpture has special meaning for the owners whose entrance it enhances. It is personal—it's their signature.

place, such as the entry foyer, give a proud emphasis to these achievements.

Is there an artist in your family who can create something expressive and beautiful for the new house? One lady, a gifted potter, made ceramic tiles for her kitchen counter and backsplash, decorating them with a Mexican theme reflecting the country she and her husband had visited on their honeymoon. Another lady, using the same medium of expression, created tiles to face the living room fireplace. Each tile commemorated a family event—birth, marriage, graduation, promotion, and the like.

Although few of us are creative artists, every family has objects that evoke many emotions and deserve a place in the home. These things may not be beautiful to anyone else, but they are much more expressive of the individuals within a home than the sterile clichés for sale in decorators' studios. Add a meaningful signature to your home by using your treasure whether it's a framed watercolor by your five-year-old to brighten your kitchen, your teenager's wrestling trophy, or the wheel from the wagon your great grandfather drove West, wired for use as the family room light.

5

HOUSEKEEPING AND MAINTENANCE

"Domestic help is a thing of the past," the professor said, as she gave the grand tour of her new home. "I'm at the college all day, and I don't want to spend every free moment cleaning house," she continued, as she pointed out numerous features planned and built into her home to keep household chores to a minimum. She spoke the sentiments of all who find housecleaning a drag but like a clean house. Resourceful persons can find more productive things to do with their years than scrubbing floors, so the more work-saving devices, the better.

A little thought about how the house is to be used, who is to do the work, and what soil it will be subjected to can help in planning many work-saving aids at little or no extra cost. More costly items can be weighed against their usefulness, and you may decide they are worth their additional dollars in time and even tempers.

Think of the flow of work and traffic throughout the house. If all groceries, supplies, cleaning equipment, parcels, Christmas trees, and furniture must be carried up a narrow spiral stair, its unique aesthetic qualities suddenly grow dim. Likewise, if you must walk a mile from the kitchen to the freezer, then it would seem that the freezer wasn't planned for. Or if you must constantly clean clay and paint from the carpet in the children's room, then it would appear that the flooring was wrong. However, you should never sacrifice all beauty for practicality, because as one great philosopher pointed out, man's ultimate aim is the acquisition of beauty.

A home serves aesthetic and functional purposes, and there should be a balance between these entities in proportion to the value *you*

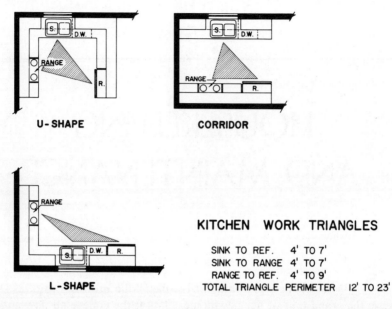

U- SHAPE   **CORRIDOR**

L - SHAPE

KITCHEN WORK TRIANGLES

SINK TO REF.   4' TO 7'
SINK TO RANGE 4' TO 7'
RANGE TO REF.   4' TO 9'
TOTAL TRIANGLE PERIMETER   12' TO 23'

To make your kitchen efficient and less fatiguing, the work triangle—the distance the homemaker must walk so often from refrigerator to sink to stove—must not exceed 23 feet. Any shape of kitchen can have an efficient work triangle, as shown in these three illustrations. (Courtesy of W. D. Farmer, Residence Designer, Inc.)

place on them. A home in which all emphasis has been placed on the beautiful can become a burden to live in and care for, as expressed by the lady of one of the South's loveliest ante-bellum homes, "I've had all the luxuries, but none of the comforts of life." She sat among Meissen figurines and Louis XIV furniture, marble mantels, and silver doorknobs and hinges as she spoke. Yet the care and maintenance of it all required her total energy. Her home completely dominated her, and she had scarcely a moment to realize and enjoy the beauty surrounding her.

No more fortunate is the occupant of a dwelling that is completely utilitarian without the occasional relief of beauty. The oppressive, sterile, monotony found in barracks, hospitals, and dormitories is efficient and functional and serves well at certain times in our lives, but it does not provide background for creative living. As you plan your home, keep in mind the value *you* put on beauty and efficiency in your family's mode of living. Think of the work that must be done and the movement of traffic throughout the house. Try to achieve a balance that will make the home a joy for every family member to live in daily.

Mentally "live" in your new home through a normal day's activities and pinpoint any problems of housekeeping. Maybe your teenager comes through after working on his "wheels," leaving a trail of greasy handprints, and your toddlers sneak animal crackers to the doggie under the bed. Project yourself into different seasons of the year to anticipate the effects of geography and climate. Perhaps Dad will stamp snow from his boots after walking home from the bus, or Mom will bring in red clay from the camellia garden. Do molds and algae grow rampant in the hot season in spite of all the chemicals you buy, and do those creepy, crawly things spontaneously generate and march around the kitchen at night?

Be realistic in anticipating trouble spots, remembering to include all members of the household—feathered, furred, and finned. Pets of some kind (and their newspapers, odors, stains, and hair) are found in almost every home. Although pet accidents never can be totally eliminated, planning the location of their feeding, sleeping, and bathroom areas can make the cleanup easier. Children make messes too, and as they grow their messes change from one kind to another. Provisions should be made for their future activities as well as the present ones.

Twentieth-century technology has produced many things to make housecleaning simpler. Almost every interior surface of your new home can be finished with a plastic-coated material that merely wipes clean. Washable wallpaper, paneling, and paint are available at little or no extra cost. Floors no longer must be scrubbed and waxed weekly; "no-wax" surfaces can be found in sheet, roll, or poured goods. Colors, patterns, and styles are endless in these products, and a wide selection is offered for any style of decoration. Neither decor nor cost need be a limiting factor here. Windows no longer have to be a headache to clean, causing you to hang precariously out the second floor to reach the outside panes. All styles can be purchased with sections that lift, turn, or flip into position to be washed.

If you really want to devote a smaller portion of your life to cleaning house, then evaluate the cost, usefulness, and energy consumption of some appliances that easily can be built in now but would be quite costly to install later. An electronic air cleaner should be first on your list because it not only provides innumerable health benefits (discussed in Chapter 12), but it prevents air-borne dust and dirt from accumulating, thus drastically cutting down the frequency of dusting and vacuuming. A central vacuum can be installed with outlets in every room to eliminate lugging a machine from room to room. Garbage disposers, trash compactors, self-cleaning stoves, and frostless refrigerators and freezers are kitchen marvels that help liberate housekeepers from old-fashioned drudgery and free them to expend their energies in more enjoyable pursuits.

Approximate Energy Consumption of Housekeeping Appliances

Item	Average Wattage	Approximate Annual Consumption in Kilowatt Hours
Electronic air cleaner	50	216
Garbage disposer	445	30
Freezer (15 cu. ft.)	341	1,195
Frostless freezer (15 cu. ft.)	440	1,761
Refrigerator (12 cu. ft.)	241	728
Frostless refrigerator (12 cu. ft.)	321	1,217
Stove (standard oven)	12,200	1,175
Stove (self-cleaning oven)	12,200	1,205
Vacuum cleaner	630	46
Central vacuum cleaner	647	49

Your kitchen should receive very special attention in your plans because the activity of this room affects every family member at some time every day. It's the nerve center of the home, and it must work efficiently and be planned to meet the needs of your family. It doesn't matter whether you are nibblers (existing primarily on convenience foods, handheld and grabbed on the run), or whether your style is a seven-course dinner with candles and wine. Your kitchen should be tailor-made to your family's activities. How much counter space do you need? Most ready-built homes have very little, and the cooks find themselves constantly moving things from one point to another to clear an area large enough for work. What about kitchen storage space? Do you find the standard floor and wall cabinets adequate and convenient? Do they hold the size cereal boxes you buy? Perhaps a pantry with adjustable open shelves would be better suited to your needs. How often is the marketing done? If it's once a month now to economize on gasoline, you need far more food and supply storage space than when it was twice weekly. Do you pull strudel, or make enchiladas, or fill your freezer from your own backyard vegetable garden? Or maybe you don't

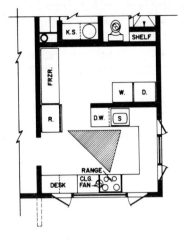

In addition to an efficient work triangle of 20 feet, the authors' kitchen and pantry accommodate a large freezer, storage shelves, washer, and dryer within easy reach. Twenty-one linear feet of counter space and a kitchen phone complete the work center, reducing the distance the homemaker must walk to perform utilitarian tasks, yet providing a spacious area to work in. (Courtesy of W. D. Farmer, Residence Designer, Inc.)

have time for anything more than popping a few things in a microwave oven. Whatever your family's style is—plan for it.

To improve efficiency in your daily work, the storage and arrangement of things you use should be planned systematically. First, list all your activities and divide them into three categories:

1. Those done frequently

2. Those done occasionally

3. Those done rarely

Next, list everything needed to perform each activity. Last, plan and arrange the area where each activity is performed, so that those things needed frequently are most easily reached, those used occasionally are in less accessible spots, and those needed rarely are located in the least convenient places. *Hand and body movements should always be kept at a minimum.*

Using these principles in planning storage and general arrangement of furniture and appliances, you'll find that the freezer should be in the kitchen or pantry, not the basement or carport. Clothes closets should be in bedrooms, not down a 30-foot hallway in the entrance foyer as we found in one home we visited. The washer and dryer shouldn't be three floors away from the nursery, and linens should be stored where they are used. It really doesn't matter, however, if you have to crawl on hands and knees through the attic space to find the holiday decorations—it will happen only once a year.

Housekeeping is more than just housecleaning—it includes all the motions that must be made to do all the things that must be done. Simplicity of design can cut down the number of doors that must be opened and corners that must be turned. Every superfluous niche or alcove provides more corners for cobwebs, and ornate trims are dust catchers. Any unnecessary motions your family must make to perform daily routines contribute to fatigue and frayed tempers. Plan so your home will be a pleasure to everyone daily.

6

LOOK AT MATERIALS

Nothing stimulates your creative imagination so much as seeing the great variety of building materials available for your choosing—colors, textures, designs, and shapes you have never seen before! One item may activate a whole new concept of thinking. An example might be a cherry red basin that could spark an entirely fresh idea for your son's bath and adjoining bedroom. A large, sculptured tile could stimulate you to design an extraordinarily beautiful fireplace wall. A sparkling crystal chandelier might be the one missing factor in your mental picture of your entrance foyer, and seeing it in a showroom could suddenly cement together all your ideas into one, gracious unity.

Surveying the entire building materials market will not only stimulate your thinking; it will let you see the complete offerings available for your selection. Many prospective homeowners' thinking is limited to those materials they have seen in ready-built houses. Builders must lean toward moderation in their selection and use those items that will please the majority of the people. You seldom see a house built for sale with bright colors or bold designs, and when you do, it will likely remain on the market far longer than the one next door in which everything is understated. Because you are not trying to please the majority of the people but only yourself, you want to see *all* first. Then if you choose the builder's model, it will be because you choose it from all available, not because you thought it was the only thing available.

You will quickly learn that manufacturers offer three price ranges in almost every item—bottom-, middle-, and top-of-the-line model.

Visit display rooms and select colors, textures, and designs for each area of your house.

Herein lies the greater part of your sleuthing because *price and quality do not necessarily correlate*. Bottom-of-the-line items may be cheaper because they are imported from countries with cheap labor. The quality may be identical or better than higher priced middle-of-the-line American made models. This is particularly true of plywood paneling and ceramic tile. Surprisingly, you may find that a manufacturer has put the same essential working parts in all three lines and has created a price difference by adding gadgetry. Appliances often fall into this category, and you must decide how often you would really use a meat thermometer that automatically turns off the oven, or the three extra cycles of the dishwasher, and if they are worth the additional cost. Price and quality do correlate sometimes: you may find plumbing fittings in which the top-of-the-line carries a lifetime warranty against leaking, the middle-of-the-line a 10-year warranty, and the bottom-of-the-line is sure to leak as soon as its short warranty has expired.

Price is subject to the fickleness of fashion in building materials as well as in clothing or furniture. The "in" color or design may command a higher price than the "out" one but not be of superior quality. When knotty, exterior siding is fashionable, its price is greater than the unblemished, even though some experts cite its quality as inferior because knots fall out and give access to insects and water. On the other hand, long-time mass demand of the same item can bring its price down, as found in pricing bathtubs. The standard, full-size model is cheaper even though it contains more material and is heavier to transport than a smaller square one. Part of your task in looking at materials is to find out *why* the price is what it is. Does it really reflect the quality, or is it merely a function of fashion and demand?

Relative cost is the difference between the cost of an alternate item and the one usually used. When you are quoted a price of $2.75 per foot for wide plank flooring, you have no way of knowing whether that's cheap or expensive unless you also know that $2.25 per foot is the price for a standard hardwood floor. Therefore, even though you may not plan to use some of the standard things in your home, price them to obtain the relative cost of your favorites. In this way you might find that the relative cost of a $250 sliding glass door would be only $20 because the brick and wood normally used for the wall would cost $230.

There may be temporary shortages of some items caused by the manufacturer's difficulties in obtaining necessary raw materials, or delivery slowdowns and strikes may hold up supplies. To avoid frustration and delays in your home, select a second and third choice—discussing with the supplier the chance of prompt delivery at building time.

Stone combines well with glass and wood. Decorative stone is repeated in the landscaping reflected in the window.

46

As you thumb back through your collection of magazine pictures, you may realize that something you had your heart set on isn't available on the local market. What then? Your builder will prefer doing business locally, but he will be glad to special order some items. Ordering, however, often involves delays and should be done with temperance. If you insist on ordering essentials (or a great number of other things) from far distant sources, prepare for long periods of idleness at the building site.

When looking at materials, it will be helpful if you make a chart to use in comparing and remembering what you see. Have a column for each of the following characteristics:

IDENTIFICATION   Record all identification—brand name, model number, style, name, and color. Find out how often new models are issued and if the one you are looking at will be available at building time.

DO YOU LIKE IT?   Your automatic subjective opinion is the most important one. If your answer is "no" or "maybe," then keep looking.

ASSETS   Include those things that would be an advantage in your home.

LIABILITIES   List here the qualities that could cause you dissatisfaction.

MAINTENANCE   How much maintenance will be required? By you, or a specialist? At what cost? Is there any kind of warranty or guarantee?

REPLACEMENT   With normal use, how soon will it have to be replaced? Will that be complicated or costly? Can you do it yourself?

USE   What is its normal use? Can it be used innovatively?

RELATIVE COST   What is the cost as compared with the commonly used material? (Your proximity to sources of supply might change this from the following chart. For example, if you live near a slate quarry you might mark slate's relative cost "low.")

INSTALLATION COST   How does the labor cost compare to that of the commonly used material?

Use this chart as a starting point and expand it with the details of your findings.

Item	Identification	Do You Like It?	Assets	Liabilities
Flooring				
Hardwood			Can be stained variety of colors; adds stability to floor	Noisy if not covered with rugs; absorbs moisture and stains
Carpeting			Continuous expanse can unify and enlarge floor space; absorbs sound; feels warm under foot	Depends on fiber and weave
Slate			Luxurious appearance; long wear	Heavy; requires concrete slab or extraordinary support; easily scratched; cold under foot; tiring to stand on for extended periods
Poured Plastic			Nonallergic; low maintenance; does not show wear	Slippery when wet; moderate selection of colors
Vinyl Asbestos Tile			Low cost; long wear	Patterns often too "kitcheny" or institutional for wide use; constant maintenance
Wall Covering				
Paint			Low cost; wide range of colors	Easily soiled; can be monotonous
Paper			Wide range of colors and patterns	Designs discontinued; easily soiled
Paneling			Variety of designs and colors; adds warmth and luxury	High cost; sometimes difficult to match or stack

Maintenance	Replacement	Use	Relative Cost	Installation Cost
Occasional cleaning and waxing; refinishing 5–7 years	Never	Anywhere except humid or stain-prone areas	Moderate	Moderate
Regular vacuuming; occasional home cleaning; professional cleaning 1–2 years	5–10 years	Anywhere except music room; specific kinds for specific areas	Low to High	Moderate
Regular vacuuming or mopping; can be sealed; refinished 5–10 years	Never	Indoors or outdoors; not recommended for children's areas	Expensive	Expensive
Occasional attention; can be patched; resurfaced 5–10 years	Never	Anywhere except bathrooms	Expensive	Expensive
Requires regular cleaning and waxing	5–15 years depending on thickness	Anywhere	Low	Moderate
Only limited washing possible	1–3 years	Anywhere	Low	Moderate
Limited washing unless treated	1–5 years	Anywhere	Moderate to High	High
Low maintenance, especially vinyl coated	10–15 years or longer	Anywhere (even baths and kitchens)	Moderate to High	Moderate

Item	Identifi-cation	Do You Like It?	Assets	Liabilities
Exterior Materials				
Redwood Siding			Resistance to weather and insects; appearance	High cost; splits easily in installation; some maintenance if painted or stained
Brick			Fire resistant; appearance	Permanently shows bad workmanship, change of crews and mortar
Fir Paneling			Low cost; ease of installation; variety of colors (paint or stain) and patterns available	Some maintenance
Stone			Fire resistant; appearance	Difficult to lay well; requires craftsmen; high cost

Maintenance	Replace- ment	Use	Relative Cost	Installa- tion Cost
Can be allowed to weather naturally; painted or stained surfaces refinished 5–7 years	Never	Walls; decks	High	High
None	Never	Walls, chim- neys, accents, walks, drives	Moderate to High	Moderate to High
Refinished 7–10 years	Never	Walls, accents	Low to Moderate	Low to Moderate
None	Never	Walls, chim- neys, accents	Low to High	High to Very High

7

LIGHTING

Your lighting system is basically functional—but it can be much more. It can create another exciting dimension in your home environment, one that represents your personality and individuality. And carefully planned imaginative lighting can use even less electricity than ordinary lighting.

You can install the standard ceiling globe with a switch inside the door. You flip the switch and the room is flooded with light. Flip it again and it's dark. This is the type Edison invented; it provides illumination. But why not have more than just the practical, functional utility? Create atmosphere, moods, and special effects in addition to achieving the basic functional purpose.

Whatever your style is, design your lighting to fit and complement that style, and select compatible lighting fixtures. Styles and types of fixtures available are endless, and it's only a matter of searching and selecting to achieve lighting compatible with your decor in each room. Lighting can and should mean more than the old concept. Use it as a decorating medium, and give it the same attention and consideration you do your furnishings.

When you need light, you switch it on and there it is. Often it isn't quite enough for the job you're doing, or it isn't in the right place, and you have to bring an extra lamp or move elsewhere. This can be different in your new home. Now is the time to use a little thought and planning to change anything in your system that you don't like.

What are your lighting needs? Mentally "live" in each area of your home throughout the year and note the activities of each family member. Then decide how much and what kind of illumination is needed for each activity, remembering that the amount of natural light available differs each season and hour of the day. Taking one area at a time, your notes might read as follows:

CHILD'S AREA

Activities

- Sleeping
- Dressing
- Playing
- Studying
- Resting

How Do These Activities Change During the Year?

- Sleeping—No change
- Dressing—No Change
- Playing—Little time will be spent playing in summer. During winter much playing will be indoors because of bad weather and early darkness.
- Studying—Little will be done during summer vacation but will occur nightly when school is in session.
- Resting—No change

What Lighting Is Needed To Meet These Needs?

- Sleeping—Night light
- Dressing—Full illumination throughout the entire room
- Playing—Full illumination and special accents
- Studying—Lighting on desk and reading areas
- Resting—Soft light

As you will notice, activities change throughout the year, but even greater changes occur from year to year. Most dramatic of all are the changes in a child's area as it evolves through many stages from his babyhood to maturity. Obviously, different ages and their corresponding activities will indicate changes in furniture and decor that you will readily make, but what about lighting needs? Anticipate future needs and prepare for them during initial construction. A child will need light for reading in bed, using a microscope, typing, writing, and endless other processes of learning. His needs for electrical wall outlets will increase too when he has to plug in his electric razor, stereo, typewriter, electric guitar, and all the other paraphernalia of growing up. (Also install a covered telephone outlet in the nursery that will later become the teenager's extension phone.)

With your list of needs at hand, start thinking of the best ways each one can be met. In the child's area, where should the night light be located? How will you provide for complete illumination—two, three or four ceiling lights? What about a desk light for study? Perhaps an adjustable wall lamp would be perfect, and for soft light maybe a single recessed fixture controlled by a dimmer switch would create a restful atmosphere for listening to music and thinking. Turned to minimum illumination, this could also serve as the night light. When all needs appear to be met, reexamine the total area to see if your plan will really work. Is there enough light where you want it? Remember, you cannot solve the problem of too little light by simply inserting larger bulbs, because wiring and heat tolerances of fixtures limit the maximum safe wattage.

Where will you place light switches? They should be convenient and safely out of reach of toddlers. If you don't like to enter a dark room, don't. Locate switches so you can light an area before entering. This is especially important for stairwells, basements, storage rooms, foyers, and garages. Multiple switches for one light are handy and allow you to extinguish the lights of an area when you leave through a door different from the one you entered. Do you read in bed but hate getting up to turn out the light? Place a wall lamp over your bed and its switch within arm's reach. If you hear a suspicious noise outside and must stumble downstairs to the front door to switch on the security lights, their purpose may be defeated. Instead, place the switch in the master bedroom. Do you remember the noisy clicks old switches made? You can still get the old kind, but for the same price you can have silent ones, and for a few dollars more you can have dimmers.

Consider the replacement of bulbs too. Can you reach all fixtures or will the beautiful stairwell chandelier remain extinguished for a year because nobody can reach it?

Prepare now for lights that you plan to add later along the walk, pool, or barbecue pit. If you plan to have ceramic lanterns made for your garden path, have electricians install wiring and switches at the

(a)   (b)

(c)

You can control the placement of your electrical outlets: (a) waterproof
outside outlets should be placed by the front door for holiday lights, on
the deck, on the patio, and around the pool; (b) if you want your outlets
convenient but inconspicuous, place them low; (c) outlets can be placed
in the floor if necessary.

garden door during initial construction when it will be a simple matter. Will you someday change a back corner of the basement into a photographic dark room or shop? If so, install circuits in that area now.

How many wall outlets do you need? Plan them for all your known needs and then add more. Don't plan on extension cords (which toddlers love to cut)—especially in nurseries and around pools! Give special thought to kitchen outlets, including a separate circuit for the freezer to eliminate the possibility of overloading the circuit and subsequent loss of power which could endanger your stored food.

What are some specific lighting features that you may consider for your home? Appraise the following as individual items or as components in more complex systems:

1. Dimmers (Energy Savers)

    To control the amount of illumination from a single or multiple unit of bulbs.

2. Recessed Lights

    To eliminate fixtures, avoid breaking visual lines, and save wall space.

3. Spot Lights

    To emphasize objects or areas.

4. Permanent Wall and Ceiling Lights

    To save floor and wall space.

5. Variety of Bulbs (Lamps)

    Fluorescent (energy savers), clear, smoked, and tinted.

6. Luminous Ceilings (Energy Savers)

    Especially in dressing room and kitchen.

Examine displays at your lighting supply dealer and your local power company to see how effective these features can be. Contemplate a wider use of fluorescent bulbs because they produce four times more light from a given amount of electricity than do incandescent bulbs.

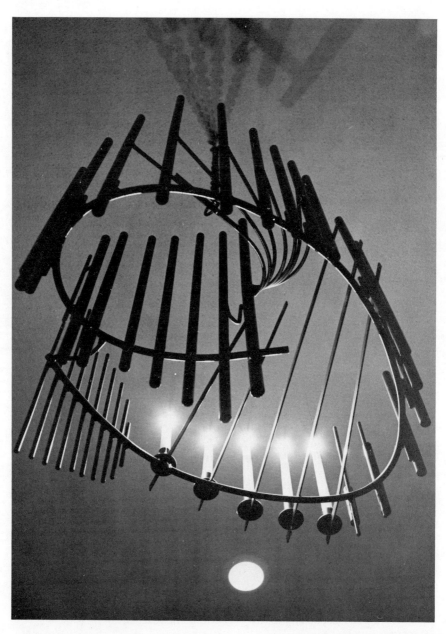

Lighting can be aesthetic while being functional. A handmade chandelier over the dining table is supplemented by recessed ceiling lights controlled by dimmer switches.

The cost of your lighting system will be based on two items: the number of receptacles and outlets installed and the price of the fixtures. A completely satisfying, unique system need not be expensive if you plan carefully what you want, where you want it, and then shop shrewdly for fixtures. Relative cost should be considered also, because spending extra money on permanently installed lights may be cheaper in the long run than buying tables and lamps to do the same job.

The power economy of your system will depend primarily on your efficiency in planning and placement. By carefully analyzing your real needs, you can avoid overlighting your home. Light intensity diminishes rapidly as it travels farther from its source, and therefore, the closer you can place your lights to the areas where illumination is needed, the less power will be used. However, the total success of this phase of home energy conservation, like all others, depends on your prudent use of it once you are living in your home.

Conservation need not mean aesthetic austerity. A contemporary home was built with walls of insulating glass, allowing the owners to live in the midst of nature within a controlled environment. Throughout the day no artificial light is needed—soft natural light floods every room. No fixtures obstruct the eye as it scans the endless vistas through expanses of glass from floor to ceiling. The effect is one of uninterrupted space. At night the home becomes another world illuminated by artificial light from recessed fixtures. The atmosphere is one of calm, relaxing, even light. Intensity is controlled by dimmers in each room, and one can experience a wide range of moods by merely turning a dial. A large candle chandelier hangs over the dining area, and recessed in the ceiling are dimmer controlled lights, ready to supplement the candles unobtrusively if needed. Such things create a different, refreshing, and exciting mood. The personality of each room is created and controlled by the turn of a dial or the flip of a switch. This is good lighting design —a system integrated into the total design and decor of the home while being economical with energy consumption.

8

ENERGY CONSERVATION

     Energy conservation is a new challenge for Americans but one that can be solved with thought and ingenuity—those time honored American attributes from which our way of life sprang. Necessity has been the "mother of invention" for over 300 years of American history, as our forefathers built the foundations for our present mode of living. We enjoy the fruits of their labor, and now we must conquer an energy shortage so that we may continue to enjoy our present way of life (and preserve it for our descendants).

     Shortages of anything—money, time, or energy—cause careful evaluation of real needs, which inevitably results in more pleasurable, efficient, and beneficial use of the short commodity. Shortages cause us to explore new avenues of satisfaction; therefore, in coping with the energy shortage as you plan your new home, you will be compelled to consider new ideas of design, materials, and equipment. These will not only conserve energy but reward your careful efforts with savings in your utility bills and create new dimensions of daily living.

Heat Loss and Gain

     Heat is lost in winter and gained in summer through all exterior surfaces of your house. Thus, the first step toward more efficient use of your heat or air conditioning energy is to reduce the exterior surface area of your house—not its size. How can this be done? By using geometry. A sphere is the geometrical shape with the smallest surface area in relation to its volume, and a cube has the next smallest surface.

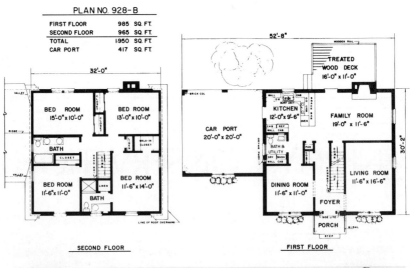

PLAN NO. 928-B

FIRST FLOOR	985 SQ. FT.
SECOND FLOOR	965 SQ. FT.
TOTAL	1,950 SQ. FT.
CAR PORT	417 SQ. FT.

SECOND FLOOR

32'-0"

BED ROOM
15'-0" x 10'-0"

BED ROOM
13'-0" x 10'-0"

BATH

CLOSET

WALK-IN
CLOSET

BED ROOM
11'-6" x 11'-0"

BED ROOM
11'-6" x 14'-0"

BATH

LINEN

LINE OF ROOF OVERHANG

FIRST FLOOR

52'-8"

30'-2"

TREATED
WOOD DECK
16'-0" x 11'-0"

KITCHEN
12'-0" x 9'-6"

FAMILY ROOM
19'-0" x 11'-6"

CAR PORT
20'-0" x 20'-0"

BATH &
UTILITY

DINING ROOM
11'-6" x 11'-0"

LIVING ROOM
11'-6" x 16'-6"

FOYER

PORCH

The more nearly your house resembles a cube in shape, the smaller will be its surface to transfer costly heat to the out-of-doors. To use this cube principle, you should minimize the number of projections, peninsulas, and wings. Your floor plan should approach a square in shape, and larger houses should be multistory rather than being long, rambling ranches.

62

ALTERNATE OMITTING
BASEMENT
FOR PLAN NO. 549

PLAN NO. 549

HOUSE	1598 SQ. FT.
CAR PORT & STORAGE	510 SQ. FT.
PORCH	54 SQ. FT.

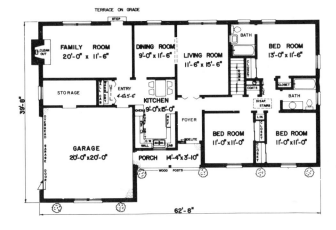

Because style is created by exterior design and materials, the cube principle does not limit your choice of style, as illustrated by the wide variety of elevations for these plans. (Courtesy of W. D. Farmer, Residence Designer, Inc.)

Spherical houses are not yet practical, but cubical houses have been a reality for centuries, and a cubical house gives the greatest living space in relation to the exterior surface area of walls and roof. Therefore, *the more nearly your house resembles a cube in shape, the smaller will be its surface to transfer costly heat to the out-of-doors.* To use this principle, you should minimize the number of projections, peninsulas, and wings. Your floor plan should approach a square in shape, and larger houses should be multistory rather than long, rambling ranches. Employing the cube principle in your design also gains substantial savings in material and labor costs, because every additional corner, angle, or projection takes more man hours and materials, and consequently more dollars, to construct.

A *two-story* house 30 feet by 30 feet with 8-foot ceilings, has 1,800 square feet of interior living space and 2,820 square feet of exterior surface. A *one-story* house having the same living space (1,800 square feet), and measuring 30 feet by 60 feet with 8-foot ceilings, has 3,240 square feet of exterior surface—*15 percent more*—including a roof area *double that of the first house!*

Heat rises and constantly buffets the roof area in its effort to escape in winter, and in summer the roof is again bombarded by intense sun heat trying to enter your home. Therefore, any reduction in roof area contributes measurably to energy conservation. The same factors affecting heat efficiency also affect air conditioning efficiency, because one is merely the reverse process of the other. During the heating season, you want to prevent heat leaving your house, and in the air conditioning months you want to prevent heat entering it.

General design, as well as shape, affects your use of energy. A wide roof overhang shades your home from severe summer sun when the rays bear down from a high angle close overhead, and yet it allows the warming rays to bathe your walls and windows in winter, when the more distant sun sends its rays at a lower angle. Floor plans that allow seldom-used portions of your home—guest rooms, shops, studios—to be shut off and unheated while unused will be advantageous. Avoid rooms that project over windswept carports or walkways. These rooms are exposed on three sides, top and bottom, and usually are farthest from the furnace.

Protect your home from cold, sweeping winter winds by walls or windbreaks of shrubs or trees. Avoid large glass areas on the windy side (usually north). Design your living areas away from hot afternoon summer sun by placing the garage on the west side if possible, and utilize trees for wind and sun protection. A tree-shaded house can be

PLAN NO. 871

FIRST FLOOR	1301	SQ. FT.
SECOND FLOOR	576	SQ. FT.
TOTAL	1876	SQ. FT.
GARAGE	494	SQ. FT.
PORCH	130	SQ. FT.
SUN DECK	160	SQ. FT.
BASEMENT	870	SQ. FT.

FIRST FLOOR

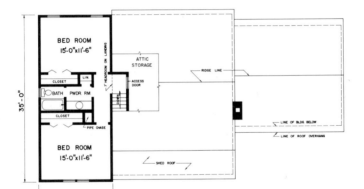

SECOND FLOOR

Floor plans allowing seldom-used portions of your home to be shut off and unheated while they are unused will help conserve heat. In this plan, the second floor bedrooms, which could be used as guest rooms, library, or studio, can easily be shut off. (Courtesy of W. D. Farmer, Residence Designer, Inc.)

65

ten degrees cooler in summer than an identical, unshaded one, and selection of a wooded site can eliminate the need for air conditioning completely, or at least considerably reduce the amount of energy required to keep your house comfortably cool.

Your choice of materials also influences your heat loss and gain, and therefore your energy needs. A light-colored roof reflects sun rays; a dark roof absorbs them and transfers the heat into your home. Brick veneer exterior walls lose 30 percent more heat than do wood siding walls insulated in the same manner. A ground level concrete slab floor loses four times the heat of a joist wooden floor over an unheated basement, and a double wooden floor added to the concrete slab reduces its heat loss by more than 70 percent.

Proper insulation must be placed in the exterior walls and roof to slow down heat transfer through these surfaces. Generally, three and one-half inches of fiberglass or the equivalent (R–11) in other materials is recommended in walls, and 6 inches (R–19) in the roof area; homes in extreme climates may need more. Cold air leaks at doors and windows can be stopped with weather stripping placed around the openings; better quality windows are designed with these features built in. Insulation and weather stripping are useless unless correctly installed, and like all areas of your construction, this depends on your selection of a good builder who will not only install these two items correctly but will build a tight, sound house without cracks or gaps anywhere.

Loose insulation, blown in, is often used in hard-to-reach ceiling areas. Because it eventually settles, a depth of 8¾ inches must be blown in to equal the R-19 value of a 6-inch batt.

Heat and smoke from the stove can be vented to the outside, thus diminishing the work of the air conditioner. The vent duct can be boxed in within cabinets over the hood.

Insulating glass or double glazing cuts heat loss through glass areas in half. You may use either hermetically sealed insulating glass or the cheaper unsealed double glazing without any perceptible difference in the insulating qualities of the two. Ventilating windows, fixed glass, and doors all can be made of double glass. Most major glass manufacturers make insulating glass and sell it under a trade name. Window companies offer a wide selection of styles and sizes in both insulating and double glazing. Triple glazing is available for extreme climates.

Metal window frames transfer much more heat than wooden ones, as evidenced by heavy condensation on metal frames in cold weather. Because each wood cell has a tiny air space, wood serves as an insulator, and wooden window frames will effectively cut your heat loss.

A fireplace is traditionally accepted as a source of heat, but even when in use it may be a source of heat *loss*. While a fire is burning, the fireplace rapidly draws air up the chimney—and where does that air come from? Ultimately, it must come into your home from the cold outside, either through cracks and leaks at windows and doors or from a slightly ajar window you open. Whether or not the heat produced by the fire can conquer the cold it brings in depends on how hot your fuel burns and how cold the outside air is. Even when the damper is closed, warm air continues to go up the chimney, because the damper area is neither insulated nor weather stripped, and a constant transfer of heat occurs through and around it. A fireplace does bring cheery warmth to the room it's in, but its presence in your home will often cause a heat loss.

All kitchen appliances—stove, dishwasher, refrigerator, and freezer—create heat that can be utilized in winter to heat the kitchen. Yes, even refrigerators and freezers give off heat—heat that has been removed from their contents in the chilling process. If these appliances are "frostless," they generate still more heat evaporating the condensate from the frostless coils. You may find that heat from your appliances is sufficient to warm your kitchen in winter and that you will not need any additional heat source in that room. If more heat is needed, don't place the unit near the freezer or refrigerator, because the two opposing forces will desperately fight one another and waste valuable energy.

What happens to all that appliance heat in summer? It's still there, laden with uncomfortable humidity unless you provide definite means to remove it. A fan vented to the out-of-doors can whisk it away in minutes, leaving the kitchen comfortable and relieving the burden on the air conditioner.

What Kind of Energy Should You Use?

Energy conservation is a twofold concern: to produce enough power and to prevent depletion of fossil fuels—coal, oil, and natural gas. Electricity, a major energy form, can be manufactured in several ways: by burning fossil fuels, by damming rivers (hydroelectric), by utilizing earth heat (geothermal), by harnessing nuclear power, or by converting solar energy. Only the first two, burning fossil fuels and hydroelectric power, are in wide production today although several new nuclear power plants will be in operation within a few years. Use of hydroelectric or nuclear power does nothing to deplete fossil fuels, and if electricity in your area is produced by either of these methods (call the power company if in doubt), your choice of electricity over coal, oil, or natural gas will contribute greatly to the ultimate conservation cause.

If, however, your electricity is produced by burning fossil fuels, using it instead of coal, oil, or natural gas for your heat, hot water heater, clothes dryer, stove, air conditioner, and post lanterns is a wasteful, inefficient use of basic power resources. Half the energy of the original fuel is lost in conversion of fossil fuels first to heat, next to electricity, and then back into heat or power in your home. So before you select your appliances or plan your heating system, find out how your electricity is produced. If it's by hydroelectric or nuclear means, use it for all your energy needs, but if it's produced from fossil fuels, select other kinds of energy for those items where you have a choice—heat, air conditioning, water heater, dryer, stove, and post lanterns.

Heating and Air Conditioning Systems

Whatever energy source you choose, your heating and air conditioning systems must be properly planned and installed to use your energy efficiently. Don't pinch pennies here! Buy good equipment of sufficient size to heat or cool your home in severe weather. Barely adequate machines will run constantly and wear out too soon. Plan now to have your equipment serviced regularly; it pays dividends in efficiency, comfort, and repair bills. Install automatic thermostats that turn the systems on or off as needed, and if you live in a cold region, a humidifier (which uses little power itself—approximately the same as an electric blanket), will make lower thermostat settings more comfortable, allowing you to conserve additional fuel by reducing the indoor temperature.

Locate your furnace centrally so ducts won't have to go inordinate distances to some rooms. Located in a basement room especially designed for utility systems, the furnace shown at left is easily accessible; it appears that the furnace at right was an afterthought!

To ensure good heat and cooling circulation in this high-ceilinged room, the duct opens at bottom and top. In summer, the lower vent can be closed, forcing cooled air to enter the room from the top and drop down. In winter, the upper vent will be closed, causing the hot air to enter from the bottom.

Good distribution of the heat or coolness your system produces is essential. Locate your furnace centrally so ducts won't have to go inordinate distances to some rooms. Insulate all heat and air conditioning ducts in unheated areas—basements, crawl spaces, and attics. Don't place vents, baseboard heaters, or radiators behind doors, furniture, and draperies. If you plan an area with high ceilings, place delivery and return-air vents at both floor and ceiling to maintain good circulation. Close ceiling vents and open lower ones in winter (heat rises), and close floor vents and open upper ones in summer to allow chilled air to fall.

Does your house have attic space? Placing a ventilating fan there to remove trapped, hot, summer air will reduce the work your air conditioner must do to keep your home cool. Ventilating fans in bathrooms and laundry to remove hot, steamy air in summer also reduce energy consumption of the air conditioner, because a great part of its work is condensing out excess humidity from your home's atmosphere. (If you use a humidifier during winter months, don't forget to turn it off when the air conditioning season arrives.)

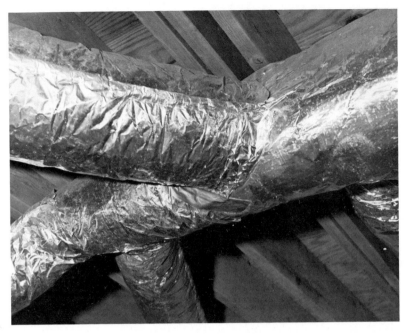

All heating and cooling ducts should be well insulated.

Lights

Candlelight is a romantic way of conserving light energy, but it's not very practical throughout the house. There are several better ways that won't create fire hazards but will add interest and excitement to your lighting design and conserve energy. Begin by placing your lights where they are really needed, not necessarily in the conventional spots. The conventional center ceiling kitchen fixture must be intense in order to get enough light to the counters, stove, and sink. Individual lights placed over these areas can provide better lighting with less electricity, and if you place them on different switches you may turn on only those needed where you are working. This principle can be employed throughout the house.

Utilize natural light for daytime lighting. Design enough windows or skylights in each area so artificial light will be unnecessary during the day, and plan your curtains and draperies to allow full use of your window light. Double glass can be used to prevent increased heat loss resulting from the additional window area. Light colored interior walls and mirrors will decrease the amount of light any area needs by day or night.

Energy-saving fluorescent lights in the ceiling and under cabinets provide work light. A decorative post lantern gives snack light.

Dimmer switches control light intensity and therefore the amount of energy used. There are many areas in your home where you might need bright light at certain times and soft light at other times. Dimmers can provide these variations of light from one fixture and conserve energy as well. You might enjoy your family room brightly lighted while having guests in for an after-game party, and softly lighted when watching television. Or perhaps you would like to turn a hall light into a soft nightlight outside the children's bedrooms.

Fluorescent bulbs produce *four times* the amount of light from a given amount of electricity as do incandescent bulbs. Thus, great energy savings can be achieved by planning the use of fluorescent lights where you might otherwise use incandescent lighting.

Conveniences

Self-cleaning ovens are the ultimate in modern conveniences, and although they use tremendous energy to do the cleaning job, their total consumption (see page 40) is only slightly more than that of a standard oven. They have heavier insulation to protect the user from the extremely high temperature required during the cleaning, and the extra insulation increases energy efficiency during cooking. The same effect of effortless oven cleaning is achieved in other ovens by using treated interior surfaces, slide-out panels, or foil liners, none of which consume any additional energy in the cleanup process.

Extra cycles on the dishwasher allow you to adjust the appliance's operation to the workload it has. This can save energy used for hot water production as well as that used to run the machine when the load is a light one.

Microwave ovens reduce cooking time by about 75 percent, and therefore the energy consumed in the cooking process is reduced a like amount. Such ovens can be built in to supplement your regular oven, and you might include one of these modern miracles in your energy-saving plans.

Some energy conservation devices, such as the cube principle of design, will reduce building costs. Others, such as insulating glass and microwave ovens, will add to your costs, but even they will ultimately pay for themselves in savings on your utility bills. However, the greatest dividend you can realize from incorporating energy conservation measures into your home plans is that you can enjoy a meaningful, productive daily life—living a delightful new lifestyle—while making a worthwhile contribution to the conservation cause.

9

NEW IDEAS IN ENERGY EFFICIENCY

The previous chapter deals with principles of design and efficient use of traditional materials. This chapter explores new ideas—many still experimental but promising. All are sound in theory, practical in operation, and favorable in the judgment of building inspectors and lenders.

Solar Heat and Hot Water

"We're going to have solar heating in our new house!" the excited housewife told us when we mentioned an increase in our utility rates. She, like many others seeking relief from oppressing energy bills, was desperately trying to solve her problem. She had been "taken in" by the attractive brochures and impressive statistics of a solar heating company. Although she had no real facts about solar heating and didn't even know if it could work in her new location, the advertisement had captivated her with the promise of getting something for nothing, and so she was going to have solar heating in her new home.

About three million BTUs (British thermal units) of heat reach the roof of your house every day from the sun. Capturing part of this to heat your home and warm your bath water is possible. It may even be economically wise today, and given annually escalating utility bills it will be more attractive in the future. But solar heating is not the entire answer to the world's energy problems yet, because even though many solar installations are working successfully, solar heating is still in an experimental stage. No standard guidelines have been achieved. There is no standardization of component parts; each solar heating "expert" has his own system and materials. And there is not even agreement on the collection area or storage volume necessary for a given location.

(a)

(b)

(a) *Georgia Power Company experimental solar house, Atlanta, Georgia;* (b) *solar heat-collecting panels on the house;* (c) *this 3,000-gallon con- crete block basement water storage tank serves the solar heating system*

Many solar "consultants" are working out of garage labs, tossing around impressive ideas and turning up the thermostat to the gas furnace when someone asks for proof of their system. Solar heating, however, is the most promising new energy source, and the research must continue until it has reached a totally practical state. More solar heated homes must

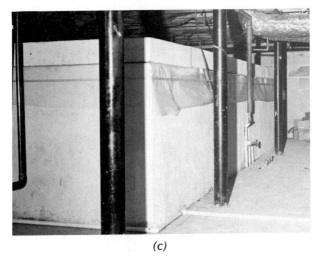

(c)

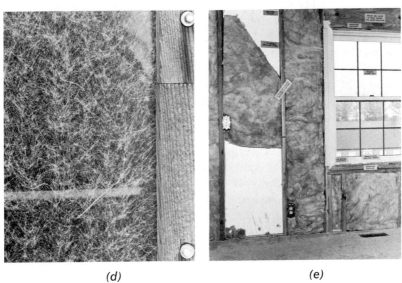

(d)   (e)

and the off-peak cooling system; (d) close-up of fiberglass-covered metal solar collector panel; (e) cutaway view showing wall insulation.

be built every year to provide more knowledge and expertise in the field.

A solar heating system consists of a collector, a storage facility, a distribution system, and a *backup heating system* (the sun cannot provide 100 percent of your heat). The collectors must face south and usually are mounted on the roof. Several different materials are being used in collector panels. No ideal material has yet been found. Some plastics are efficient collectors, but they deteriorate quickly. Glass panels are stable but are subject to breakage. Copper plates have neither of these problems but are very expensive.

Either a liquid or air is passed over the hot collectors and picks up the heat which it takes to the storage facility and transfers to the storage medium (usually water). The heat is stored until it is needed; then it is transferred to the home by the distribution system.

A backup heating system is essential because cloudy days prevent a solar system from collecting efficiently. The number of sunny days in different parts of the United States ranges from a low of 29 percent to a high of 94 percent. A solar heated home in an area where the sun shines only 29 percent of the time obviously would be cold without a backup system.

Care must be exercised in the selection of a backup heater to prevent the very thing you're trying to avoid by going to solar heating —excessive utility bills. Heat pumps are being used in conjunction with solar heating in milder climates, but usually heat pumps are not efficient in weather below 40° F. Electric heat is also used as a backup system, but power rates make it expensive in most areas.

A solar system must be custom designed for each home. The amount of sun reaching any given spot is dependent on time of day, season of the year, latitude, cloud cover, and aerial pollution. This problem is further complicated by the specific conditions of the individual lot. Is it located in a valley and shaded twice a day by hills? Is it on the north side of a hill and shaded nearly all day? Are there tall buildings or trees to the south on someone else's land that would block the sun? Would cutting your trees to create a solar window destroy valuable summer shade and therefore increase your air conditioning bill? A tree-shaded home can be ten degrees cooler in summer than an unshaded one.

Special attention must also be given to the home design so that it can accommodate a solar system. If collectors are to be placed on the roof, the pitch must be calculated for your specific latitude (generally your latitude plus ten degrees equals the necessary angle) and turned due south. If the roof area is not great enough to provide an adequate collection area, then collectors must be placed in the yard on the south side and considered in lot size and landscaping. The farther north you live, the weaker the sun, and therefore more collection area is necessary.

A solar home design must also provide an insulated heat storage area. Because most experts recommend one gallon of storage for each square foot of living space, the storage facility must accommodate over 1,000 gallons of water. Usually placed in the basement, the storage tank, like the house design, will contain the heat better if it is shaped on the cube principle. The distribution system for solar heating and for the backup heat system can be efficiently placed together to use the same ducts and blower. In addition to special considerations necessary to accommodate a solar system, the solar heated home should incorporate all energy-efficient design, insulation, and material features necessary in any other new home.

Although solar energy is free, the system is costly. How much it will cost you depends on many factors, the greatest being the cost for collectors. The collection area necessary depends on where you live and how much sun shines on your lot, the size of your home, the calculated heat loss, the temperature you desire, and the efficiency of the collectors. The substance passed over the collectors to pick up and transfer the heat may also be a cost factor. If air is used, that of course is free. Water also is cheap, but if you need other fluids to prevent freezing, these can be costly. The mechanical components, tubing, thermostat, valves, and sensors used should be stock items and therefore not expensive. Most of the installation can be done by regular plumbers, carpenters, masons, and heating contractors. High-priced specialists are not necessary in most cases. All these costs are in *addition to another complete heat system to back up the solar one.* You can expect a solar system for a 2,000-square-foot home in a medium climate to add from $6,000 to $10,000 to the building costs.

Whether solar heating is economically feasible for *you* depends on:

1.   How much a solar system will add to your building costs.

2.   What percentage of your heat a solar system can provide.

3.   How much the free heat would cost *today* if provided by another system.

4.   How much the free heat *could cost in the future* if provided by another system.

5.   How long it will take the savings to pay for the system.

An $8,000 solar system in a 2,000-square-foot Atlanta home, where winter temperatures average 45° F and range from 15° F to 65° F, could provide about 60 percent of the needed heat. At present electric rates of 3.26 cents per kilowatt hour, it would cost $652 per year to heat the home electrically. Savings from a solar system would be $391 per year, and it would take 20 years to pay for the system in electric savings at present rates. At present Atlanta natural gas rates of 17.2 cents per therm, it would cost $185 per year to heat the home with gas.

The 60 percent solar savings would be $111, and when compared to gas, it would take 72 years to pay for the system.

How fast utility costs will rise is unknown, but if they continue to rise in the future as they have in the recent past, the actual time it would take to pay for a solar system would be much less than 20 or 72 years. Because of this lenders are looking favorably on solar heated homes.

Maintenance of a solar system is relatively simple. There are few moving parts, and these are standard items—easy to service and inexpensive to replace. Deterioration and corrosion of collectors can be a problem. When you go shopping for the right system, demand a guarantee that all materials will hold up. Also demand *proof* that the system works. Visit a demonstration home on a cold day. Don't deal with any solar "expert" unless he has been in business at least two years, has several demonstration homes in operation (and welcomes your visit), and is recognized by local bankers, business people, the Better Business Bureau, and the National Association of Home Builders as being an honest, ethical person to deal with.

If you decide to pursue solar heating, you may have difficulty locating the right expert because people within the industry have not yet decided what to call themselves. They may be "solar consultants," "solar engineers," "solar energy experts," or "solar heating contractors." Your planner, builder, and the local Home Builders Association can help you locate the correct personnel.

Solar hot water systems are similar to solar heaters. Water is passed over collectors and stored in insulated tanks until needed. A backup heater is necessary for hot water too. Solar water heaters may be installed separately or in conjunction with a solar heating system and are on the market as complete units.

Solar Electricity and Air Conditioning

Converting solar energy to electricity is the ultimate goal of most solar research. When this process has been perfected and priced within reach of the average consumer, solar energy will be the answer to the world's energy problems. Much research in this direction is presently in progress by individuals, universities, and corporations. Workable generators probably will be on the market by the early 1980s. Until this occurs, solar air conditioning will not be practical.

Wind Power

Like the sun, the wind is another source of free energy available to man. For centuries windmills have captured the force of moving air and converted that energy into turning wheels, but the work produced

A solar home: top, a front view; bottom, heat collecting panels on the south roof of the home. Water circulates through copper pipes under plastic film.

by the traditional windmill was a simple form, limited to activities derived directly from the turning wheel.

Windmills have been used in recent times in rural America primarily to pump water for farm animals and home use. This effective and efficient function is still in use today, but harnessing the wind's energy for use as a major power source for a modern home is another matter. We are not concerned merely with the operation of a simple machine, but with producing the energy needs for all the things that keep a modern home functioning—heating and cooling, lighting, cooking, and running numerous appliances. This means that the wind-turned wheel is of no direct value but must be used to produce electricity—the power form common to all the needs of a home.

Don't think you can buy a windmill and solve all your energy problems while others watch their commercial utility bills climb. Like solar heating systems for the home, wind power has its limitations. Research is progressing, and in the future effective wind generators may be developed that will answer many energy problems. However, for now wind-powered generator systems available for producing electricity for the home are not the practical, realistic solution most people seek.

Modern wind-driven power plants do not look at all like traditional windmills. Most of them have two or three blades mounted on a tower resembling a TV transmitter. Wind turns the propellers that operate the electric generator. Electric current can feed directly into your appliances (dc), or if ac power is desired, a dc-to-ac electric inverter is required. Electricity can be stored in batteries for future use. Wind plants are sophisticated scientific machines.

A wind generator might be a useful *supplemental* electric power source for your home if your specific needs, home, and location are suitable. Get your answers to the needs and requirements for an effective system *before* you plan to install any type of home wind plant.

Wind-driven power plants produce free electricity when the wind blows. Don't be misled by this obvious fact and race out to buy a plant because you observe that there generally is wind at your home site. The amount of electrical power produced by a wind plant is determined by the speed of the wind and the time it blows. You must acquire accurate wind data for at least one year for the exact spot you plan to locate your windmill. What is the average daily wind speed? How many days per year is there wind and for how long each day at what velocity? Without these data you may install a machine and find that the air doesn't move at a speed adequate to operate your plant enough hours per day, enough days per year, to produce a worthwhile amount of electricity.

Not every home site is suitable for a wind generator. There may not be enough wind or there may be too much. Are there frequent hurricanes, tornados or other extreme weather conditions in your area? Are there trees on your land that would block the wind from your windmill (and perhaps you don't want to cut the trees because they provide shade for the house in summer)? Are there hills or other natural or man-made barriers that would diminish your wind supply? You must acquire this information by your own research or from professional engineers. Most wind plants need from 20 to 25 mph wind to produce at capacity, and they generate little power in winds as low as 6 mph.

Wind electric systems are sized by their electrical output. A 6,000 watt system, one of the largest available, can produce 325 KWH per month in 10 mph winds. That can power a refrigerator, freezer, small appliances, and lights but not a stove, hot water heater, or air conditioner. Such a system costs over $10,000. Multiple units (at multiple prices) can be installed to produce more power.

How much power do you need every month? Look at your old electric bills to determine how many KWH you used. It's probably much more than one wind machine can produce.

There are booklets and "do it yourself" manuals on the market telling how to build a wind generator and solve your energy problems. Some even tell how to build your wind plant from parts of automobiles and other items found in junk yards, but what can such a plant produce? Usually only enough electricity to light one lamp and power a radio—when the wind blows.

The cost of a system will vary according to the amount of power you want from it and your specific location. Even though you can make your own, buy a kit, or buy a factory model, don't do anything until you have ascertained that it will work at your site. Determine how much you can get from it and what it will cost.

The wind is free and carries with it all the potential energy you need. Wind generators can capture some of that energy, convert it into electricity, store it, and light your home. But to what extent and at what cost?

Water Power

Water is another potential source of free home energy. The water-powered wheel has for centuries paralleled the wind-powered wheel. But unlike the variance of wind power, water power is usually a reliable, constant source of energy. If you have a stream on your property, it may be suitable to dam it and use it to turn a water wheel to operate an electric generator. Also a stream-fed lake or pond sometimes can be channeled to operate a water wheel. Once the water wheel is built and the generator installed, you can enjoy free power as long as the water flows. But like wind power, this is usually a supplemental system and may not produce all the power a normal household requires. If, however, you have water, why not use it?

Before you buy or build a water generator system, have a civil engineer determine how much electricity your water is capable of producing. Compare this to your electrical needs. Only then can you evaluate the feasibility of installing a home hydroelectric plant. Every flowing stream or body of water is a potential source of power. But what is the least amount worth developing? You must know the potential power of your water to decide if it is economically feasible.

Also you must know if the water is present all year. A swift stream may diminish to a trickle in later summer or become a torrent and overflow its banks at other times. Once a water power plant is set in operation, there is continuous production of electricity as long as the water flows as you predicted.

What are your electrical needs? A home hydroelectric plant may not supply all of them, but it can supply some and reduce the amount of electricity you must buy. And it can be invaluable as an emergency power source if your commercial supply fails temporarily. Calculate your monthly electrical needs, determine the output to expect from your generator, research the total cost for installing the system, and see what the results indicate. You may find that you would never regain the cost of the plant in electrical savings, or you may discover that it would be economically sound. Don't get so carried away with the feeling of independence you gain from your own power source that you are blind to reality. Water power is real and it works (it's the power source for many commercial power companies), but whether you have enough water on your land to make it economically worthwhile is another matter.

Work with the truth of mathematics and dollars, not emotions. But after your study is completed, if the conclusions indicate that you may not be able to generate enough electricity to save money, you may still like to install a water wheel system for the satisfaction of knowing that you are doing something toward the conservation of natural resources and not wasting the energy you already have. You may also gain pleasure from building your own plant and watching it produce the light by which you figure how to pay for it.

Fireplaces

Ninety percent of the heat generated in the traditional fireplace goes up the chimney. Warmth felt as you sit by the fireside comes to you as heat rays radiated from the fire. The greater part of the heat generated warms the air around the fire, creating a draft and drawing air into the

(a)

(b)

(a) *Fireplace heat collector: water-carrying pipes under and behind the grate collect heat for storage and distribution through the central heating system.* (b) *Water storage tank for the fireplace heat collector: hot water heated in the fireplace is stored in this tank and passed through a heat exchanger installed in the furnace system.*

fire from the room and rapidly sending hot air up and out the chimney. Cold air to feed the fire enters the home by infiltration around doors and windows. When the fire is out, warm room air continues to escape through the damper. The real value of the traditional fireplace is mostly aesthetic and psychological—not as an efficient heat source.

Energy awareness has spurred research, changing the fireplace from a mere decoration to a furnace capable of supplementing or replacing other heat sources. The simplest and cheapest alteration to your fireplace is to replace the standard grate with one made of hollow tubes. Cold air is drawn into the tubes beneath and in front of the fire. The air is heated as it goes under, behind, and over the fire, and is expelled with moderate force into the room. Much of the heat normally lost is diverted back into the room. This simple device costs about $20.

A more efficient fireplace heater is being marketed by several manufacturers of prefab fireplaces. Glass doors seal the firebox from the room, and an outside air vent provides the oxygen and draft for the fire. Cold room air is drawn through vents below the firebox, circulated around it, heated, and expelled into the room through vents at the top. Since the firebox is sealed from the room, inside air is not drawn through the fireplace from windows and doors either while the fire is burning or after it is out, as in a traditional fireplace. This fireplace in a 28-inch size costs about $600, or $250 more than a prefab without the heat-conserving features. Installation costs are about the same.

The ultimate in fireplace efficiency is one combining the sealed firebox and outside air source of the model described above with the ability to store the heat and use it to heat the entire home. For about $1,000 you can purchase and install a fireplace heat collector system in your home. This heat system consists of a grate with metal tubes running through it. Water circulated through the tubes is heated and stored in an insulated tank until it is needed to heat the home. Then it is passed through a heat exchanger attached to the blower of the central heating system, and the heated air is circulated through the home by way of the existing duct system. The originators estimate a four-hour fire can heat a 2,000-square-foot home for 24 hours on a 40° F winter day. Originally designed as a solar system backup, the fireplace heat collector can be used as a supplement to any kind of heating system. The cost is in addition to the cost of the fireplace.

Superior Insulation

In an hour, 36 BTUs per square foot can be lost from an uninsulated ceiling. Adding a six-inch fiberglass batt (R-19) cuts the heat loss to three BTUs per hour, and increasing this to ten inches of fiber-

THE ARKANSAS PLAN
(2"x6" FRAMING SYSTEM)

2"x6" STUDS - 24"O.C.

INTERIOR FINISH

VAPOR BARRIER

R-19 INSULATION (6"BATT)

1"x6" or BACK-UP CLIP

1/2" SHEATHING

EXTERIOR CORNER & WALL FRAMING

CONVENTIONAL FRAMING □

2"x4" STUDS - 16" O.C.

INTERIOR FINISH

3 1/2" FULL THICK BATT INSULATION R-13

PACK SPACE BETWEEN BLOCKING OF CORNER POST W/ INSULATION

VAPOR BARRIER

1" THICK POLYSTYRENE FOAM SHEATHING

EXTERIOR CORNER & WALL FRAMING

Two methods of constructing a wall with superior insulation (R-19). (Courtesy of W. D. Farmer, Residence Designer, Inc.)

glass (R-30) cuts the heat loss down to two BTUs per hour. Likewise, an uninsulated sidewall loses 15 BTUs per hour. A three and one-half-inch batt (R-11) reduces the wall heat loss to four BTUs, and six inches of fiberglass (R-19) allows a heat loss of only two BTUs per hour.

Over twice as much heat goes through the roof of a house as through the walls. Traditional insulation (3½ inches in walls and 6 inches in ceilings) makes dramatic reductions in heat transmission, and additional insulation continues to reduce heat loss but not at such a staggering rate. Energy efficiency, however, can be substantially improved by adding more insulation together with stopping air infiltration by caulking and weather stripping.

Because three and one-half-inch side wall insulation fits the standard two-by-four wall stud, adding more insulation poses a construction problem. Research conducted in Arkansas under the direction of the Arkansas Power and Light Company evolved the "Arkansas Plan" of construction to accommodate six-inch wall insulation. Conventional two-by-four wall studs placed 16 inches on center are replaced by two-by-six studs 24 inches on center. The resulting six-inch wall can accommodate a six-inch fiberglass batt. Each stud is notched at the bottom to form a raceway for electrical wiring, so insulation does not have to be squeezed behind the wires, halfway up the wall.

According to theory, the two-by-six construction takes less lumber and fewer man hours to pick up and use each piece, and therefore it should result in construction savings. But in practice two-by-six construction probably will cost you more. Laborers who have spent their lives doing two-by-four construction will not adjust to a new method quickly or easily. Workmen will have problems fitting doors and windows designed for two-by-four areas into two-by-six spaces. Framing men accustomed to automatically placing a stud every 16 inches will have to slow down to place one correctly every 24 inches. Nor will they look kindly on notching the studs for the electricians.

An easier and more economical alternate to the Arkansas construction is to face standard two-by-four construction with sheets of one-inch polystyrene foam sheathing. This, together with the standard three and one-half-inch fiberglass insulation, achieves the same resistance to heat loss as the six-inch insulation in the Arkansas Plan.

Resistance to heat loss (R-value) is a method of evaluating insulation and is written as R- followed by a number. The higher the number, the greater the resistance to heat loss, and therefore the better the insulation. Doubling the R-value does not cut the heat loss in half.

Floor, slab, and door insulation has been almost ignored in the past, but insulating here not only reduces heat loss in forgotten areas. It noticeably increases the comfort of your home by eliminating cold

Styrofoam panels, which fit tongue-and-groove, added outside 3½-inch fiberglass batts achieve an R-19 insulation.

floors. If you have only a limited amount of money to spend on additional insulation, it would best be spent here.

Your hot water heater is the third largest energy consumer in your home. Insulating it cuts its consumption significantly when it is located in an unheated area. For about $20 you can purchase a neat fiberglass wrapper to fit your tank. You can easily save the $20 cost in one year's operation. Placing your tank close to the point of use cuts down the distance hot water has to travel and cool along the way. Wrapping the pipes with insulation further reduces heat loss.

Infiltration, the entrance of outside air through cracks, should be kept to a minimum. In addition to weather stripping and caulking around doors and windows, caulking should also be added around electrical boxes and pipes and wiring where they enter the house. How well

Heat loss is reduced when water heaters and hot water pipes are insulated. Many materials can be used by the do-it-yourself enthusiast or neat ready-made "jackets" can be bought for the heaters.

the infiltration is cut depends more on the quality of workmanship than on the materials. A good builder is *essential* if you are to have an energy-efficient home.

All homes utilizing new ideas in energy conservation must use insulating windows because heat is lost faster through glass than through any other building material. Failing to install double or triple glazing would, in one step, defeat most of your gain from new ideas. Double glazing cuts window heat loss in half, and triple glazing cuts the remaining heat loss by 40 percent.

Natural Heating and Cooling

Even though windows lose heat, double glass areas that face south must not be overlooked as sources of natural solar warmth. Research proves there is a net heat gain, over BTUs of room heat transferred out, from solar heat radiation passed into the house through an insulated south window.

A glass area facing south and surrounded by deciduous shade trees provides an excellent "free" heat and cooling system. In summer the trees shade the glass from the sun, preventing the heat build-up inside the house that is desired in winter. As the weather cools and the leaves fall, the window is exposed to full sun, supplementing the inside heat. Heavy draperies can prevent a heat loss from these windows at night.

Off-Peak Cooling

When power is used concerns electric companies as well as *how much* is used. If everyone uses air conditioners at the same time, a peak load is created. Generating facilities must be designed to meet peak demands, or a "brown-out" occurs. Experimentation is in progress with residential air conditioning systems that cool at night during off-peak hours. Chilled water is stored until daytime when it is needed. House air is blown over chilled water coils and back through the house. Should this system prove as successful in residential use as it has in commercial and industrial installations, it would not save energy but would save money by using large amounts of electricity during cheaper off-peak hours.

Roof and Ceiling Cooling

Good designers have always been energy and cost conscious and have included in their designs features that saved homeowners money. However, during the era of cheap energy, many good ideas became obsolete. Now they are being revived and incorporated once again into home plans.

Continuous ridge vents are a renewed idea. These long vents along the ridge of the roof, installed with a continuous vent in the soffit, draw cool air in at the soffit and push out hot attic air at the roof top. Thus, a natural convection current ventilates and cools the roof continuously without using power. The speed of this ventilation is controlled by the heat build-up in the attic. The hotter the air, the faster the convection current; and likewise, the cooler the air, the slower the movement. In winter the slow movement of air through the soffit and ridge vent provides ventilation necessary to prevent decay-causing condensation on the underside of roof decking and rafters. The small amount of heat removed from the attic area by ventilation has already been lost from the house by passing through the thick roof insulation over the ceiling of the upper rooms and into the attic area.

Another powerless method of ceiling cooling is a ventilating clerestory window placed at the top of a sloped ceiling. Hot air moves up and out the open window in summer. To prevent the same effect in

Continuous soffit vent is used here together with a continuous ridge vent to cool the roof.

winter, a return air duct must be placed high in the ceiling (and of course, you must close the window).

An improvement in roof fans is one that is thermostatically operated. Placed low in the roof, the thermostat turns on the fan when the heat builds up to the set temperature. It operates automatically and consumes only a small amount of power.

Appliances

Appliance manufacturers have been ordered by the federal government to increase efficiency of all appliances by 20 percent by 1980. The more efficient models are being introduced (usually with a higher price) as they are developed, and you should ask about them when appliance shopping.

The value of using a humidifier to increase the comfort of lower winter heat temperatures has been mentioned. A new idea is the use of a dehumidifier in summer to reduce the humidity and therefore the work of the air conditioner. With the humidity lower, higher air conditioning temperatures are comfortable. And remember, of all the energy consumers in your home, air conditioning is the greatest.

Three Cardinal Factors

Many energy-saving devices are available to you. As you shop and choose which you can best afford and use, keep in mind the three cardinal factors affecting your home's energy consumption:

1. BUILDER   He must build tight—everywhere.

2. SHAPE   Exterior surfaces must be kept to a minimum.

3. INSULATION and WEATHER STRIPPING   Heat loss and infiltration must be reduced as much as you can afford.

10

ENERGY-EFFICIENT
LIVING

No matter how well you plan and build your home, if you don't practice energy-efficient living, you still won't achieve a reduction in your energy consumption. How you *use* your home is as important as how you *build* it. The greatest energy consumers are those things producing heat or cold—heating and air conditioning systems, water heaters, stoves, refrigerators, and freezers—with heating and air conditioning systems using a staggering 50 percent to 80 percent of your total energy. Water heating follows, accounting for 15 percent to 25 percent. Wise use of this equipment is especially important, and adopting an energy-efficient attitude toward all your energy consumers will prevent needless waste, yet not interfere with pleasant living.

The following charts compiled by the Georgia Power Company illustrate how an imaginary family of four uses its power in a 1,600-square-foot electric home. Each activity has several alternate lower energy means of achieving the same results, illustrating that efficiency, not austerity, is the key to low energy living. Costs are based on an average kilowatt hour price of 3.26 cents.

Heating and Cooling	KWH Per Year	Cost Per Year
Alternative #1: No insulation		
Single pane glass windows		
a. Individual room heaters and central air conditioning	39,636	$987
b. Heat pump heating and cooling	30,583	$791
Alternative #2: Some insulation		
(Ceiling: R-11, 3–3¼"; Walls: R-7, 2–2¼"; Floors: R-7, 2–2¼", single pane glass windows)		
a. Individual room heaters, central air conditioning	17,043	$445
b. Heat pump heating and cooling	13,349	$365
Alternative #3: More insulation		
(Ceiling: R-26, 7"; Walls: R-13, 3–3½"; Floors: R-11, 3–3½"; double glass windows)		
a. Individual room heaters, central air conditioning	11,760	$317
b. Heat pump heating and cooling	9,290	$264
Alternative #4: Most Insulation		
(Ceiling: R-38, 12"; Walls: R-19, 3–3½", plus 1" polystyrene; Floors: R-13, 4"; storm sash windows)		
a. Individual room heaters, central air conditioning	10,760	$291
b. Heat pump heating and cooling	8,471	$241

Comfort Conditioning	Estimated KWH Per Year	Estimated Cost Per Year
Room Air Conditioner	860	$28.04
Humidifier	163	$ 5.31
Dehumidifier	377	$12.29
Fan		
Window	170	$ 5.54
Circulating	43	$ 1.40
Rollaway	138	$ 4.50
Portable Heater	176	$ 5.74

Water Heating	Approximate KWH Per Use	Cost Per Use
Bathroom Use		
Tub Bath		
Hot water, approximately 5 gallons (hot and cold water needed to fill 4–5″ in tub)	1.3	$ .04
Shower		
Hot water, approximately 6 gallons (for a 5-minute shower)	1.5	$ .05
Kitchen and Laundry Use		
Dishwashing		
By hand		
Hot water, approximately 21 gallons per day (based on 7 gallons for 3 uses per day)	5.3	$ .17
Automatic dishwasher (per use)		
Hot water, 13 gallons	3.3	$ .11
Machine operation	.5	$ .02
Drying cycle	.5	$ .02
	4.3	$ .15
Hot water and machine operation, without drying cyle	3.8	$ .13
Clothes Washing by Machine		
Hot water, 31 gallons (for hot water wash and warm rinse)	7.8	$ .25
Hot water, 25 gallons (for hot water wash, cold rinse)	6.3	$ .21
Hot water, 22 gallons (warm wash, warm rinse)	5.5	$ .18
Hot water, 11 gallons (warm wash, cold rinse)	2.8	$ .09

	KWH	Cost
Monthly Estimate for Family of Four:		
Bathroom use	180	$5.87
Dishwashing:		
a. by hand (3 times per day)	159	$5.18
b. by machine (30 uses)	129	$4.21
Clothes washing (30 loads per month, various cycles)	200	$6.52

Home Entertainment	Estimated KWH Per Month	Estimated Cost
Television		
Color set, tube model	55	$1.79
Color set, solid state	37	$1.21
Black and white, tube model	29	$ .94
Black and white, solid state	10	$ .33
Radio	7	$ .23
Stereo Phonograph	3	$ .10

Cooking Comparisons	Estimated KWH Per Use	Estimated Cost
Oven Meal		
(chicken, acorn squash, cake)		
Manual clean oven (350°—50 minutes)	1.9	$ .06
Self-clean oven (350°—50 minutes)	1.2	$ .04
Microwave oven (32 minutes, high power setting)	1	$ .03
Chocolate Cake		
Manual clean oven (375°—30 minutes)	1.1	$ .04
Self-clean oven (375°—30 minutes)	.7	$ .02
Microwave oven (7 minutes)	.2	$ .01
Pot Roast		
Manual clean oven (325°—2 hours, 20 minutes)	2	$ .07
Microwave oven (1 hour, 40 minutes, low power)	.7	$ .02
Crock pot (3 hours, high setting)	.9	$ .03
Electric skillet (3 hours, 15 minutes)	.8	$ .03
Turkey		
Self-clean oven (325°—3 hours, 20 minutes)	2.2	$ .07
Microwave oven (1 hour, 40 minutes, high power)	1.1	$ .04
Baked Potatoes		
Manual clean oven (400°—1 hour)	1.7	$ .06
Microwave oven (14 minutes)	.4	$ .01
Toaster oven (400°—1 hour)	.5	$ .02

NOTE: The estimates above were tested by the Georgia Power Home Economists, using recommended cooking times and kitchen appliances in good working order. Condition of appliances and personal preferences will influence electricity use for cooking.

Laundry Equipment	Estimated KWH Per Month	Estimated Cost
Clothes Washer		
Hot water (30 loads, various temperature cycles)	200	$6.52
Machine operation	9	$ .30
Clothes Dryer		
30 full uses (approximately 3 KWH or $.10 per use)	90	$2.93
Hand Iron		
4 weeks' use (approximately 1½ hours weekly)	5	$ .16

Lighting	Time Used	Est. KWH Per Use	Est. Cost Per Use
Living Room			
Three 150-watt bulbs (total wattage: 450)	4 hrs.	1.8	$ .06
Bedrooms			
(estimate for 3 bedrooms) Three 60-watt bulbs per room (total wattage: 540)	6 hrs.	3.2	$ .10
Kitchen			
Four 40-watt fluorescent bulbs (total wattage: 160)	3 hrs.	.5	$ .02
Dining Room			
Three 60-watt bulbs (total wattage: 180)	2 hrs.	.4	$ .01
Bathroom			
Three 60-watt bulbs (total wattage: 180)	2 hrs.	.4	$ .01
Outdoor Light			
One 100-watt bulb	10 hrs.	1	$ .03
Estimated Average Use and Cost per Day:		7.3	$ .23

Estimated Monthly Use and Cost:	Est. KWH Per Month	Est. Cost
	219	$7.14

Refrigeration	Estimated KWH Per Month	Estimated Cost
Refrigerator		
Single door, manual defrost	54	$1.76
Two door, manual defrost	97	$3.16
Two door, frost free	150	$4.89
Side by side, frost free	180	$5.87
Models Advertised as Energy Efficient		
Two door, manual defrost	54	$1.76
Two door, frost free	84	$2.74
Freezer		
Upright, manual defrost	155	$5.05
Upright, frost free	210	$6.85
Chest, manual defrost	110	$3.59

Miscellaneous	Estimated KWH Per Month	Estimated Cost
Hair Dryer		
Blow-dry model (used once a day)	4	$ .13
Bonnet model	1	$ .03
Vacuum Cleaner	3.8	$ .12
Sewing Machine	1	$ .03
Floor Polisher	1.3	$ .04
Clock	1.4	$ .05

Following are many ways you can lower your energy consumption by boosting efficiency and eliminating waste.

Heating and Cooling

1. The recommended thermostat setting in winter is 65° to 68° F in daytime. If you are to be away for a few days, turn the thermostat down but not completely off. If you are going to be away for several hours, turn it back five degrees.

2. Lower the thermostat at night when you go to bed. A cutback of ten degrees for an eight-hour period can cut heating fuel consumption as much as 15 percent.

3. Dirty filters increase energy use. Check furnace and air conditioning systems monthly. Keep all equipment in good working condition.

4. Insulated drapery lining reduces heat loss.

5. In winter, leave draperies open on sunny days but draw them against cold at night. In summer, the opposite is true. Keep draperies closed in daytime to shut out heat.

6. Don't block registers or radiators with furniture or draperies that restrict air circulation and overwork heating equipment.

7. In summer, use appliances when air conditioning is in less demand: in early morning before the sun is high or after sundown. By adding to summer heat, appliances cause air conditioning equipment to work harder cooling your house.

8. Be sure your thermostat is in good working order. Check by hanging a thermometer next to it.

9. Close the door to the rest of the house if you open a bedroom window at night. This keeps the cold air out of other rooms and away from your thermostat.

10. If the basement, garage, and attic are unheated, keep the doors leading to them closed.

11. Shut doors to unused rooms and close off registers or radiators in them.

12. If you have a fireplace, be sure the damper is closed when it is not being used.

13. Remind the children to close the outside doors when they run in and out of the house.

14. Kitchen and bathroom exhaust fans should be run sparingly. They can exhaust 100 to 300 cubic feet of heated or cooled air per minute.

Water Heater

1. Avoid unnecessarily running hot water while shaving, cleaning utensils, or at any other time.

2.   If cool or warm water will do, use it instead of hot water.

3.   One drip per second from a hot water faucet wastes 650 gallons of water per year. So repair leaky faucets.

4.   Set the water heater thermostat at 140° to 150° F—the latter if you have an automatic dishwasher.

Washer

1.   Use the washer and dryer only when enough laundry has accumulated to make a full load. Or when washing a few items, use the small or medium load selection if your washer has one. The amounts of electricity used to run the washer and dryer are almost the same whether a small or full load is being washed.

2.   Vary the size of garments in a load to permit freer water circulation.

3.   Don't overload the machine; it reduces efficiency and may necessitate rewashing many items.

4.   Use the proper setting (small, medium, or large) for the size load you intend to wash. Use maximum wash time only for heavily soiled clothes.

5.   Before every load, washing or drying, remove the lint filter and clean it thoroughly.

6.   Much of the energy used in doing your family laundry goes to heat the wash water. When warm water will do instead of hot, use it. Some fabrics can even be washed in cold water. Read clothing labels carefully and follow the manufacturer's instructions.

7.   Avoid rewashing by presoaking and pretreating heavily stained items.

8.   Too much or too little detergent will cause inefficient cleaning.

Dryer

1.   Use permanent press and fluff cycles on your dryer for synthetic fiber garments.

2.   Don't overdry clothes. Besides using more energy than is necessary, it causes wrinkles to set in.

3. Taking permanent press garments out of the dryer as soon as the cycle is completed will usually eliminate the need to iron them.

4. Dry your clothes in consecutive loads. Energy used to bring the dryer up to the desired temperature shouldn't be allowed to go to waste.

5. Sort clothes by thickness so you won't have to run an additional cycle for only one or two slow-drying items.

Dishwasher

1. A dishwasher can use less hot water than washing and rinsing dishes by hand with running water.

2. Have a full load before running the dishwasher. This saves water, detergent, and energy to heat the water and run the dishwasher.

3. Dishwashers give off heat and humidity, so during the summer run them in the cooler morning or evening hours.

4. If the dishwasher has selections for different types of dishes, use the recommended ones for the kind of dishes or utensils being washed.

Stove

1. Thaw frozen foods at room temperature before cooking them in the oven. Starting with a frozen roast requires 65 percent more time.

2. Bake several items at one time. Freeze extra portions for future use.

3. Preheat oven only for foods requiring precise timing. Preheating isn't necessary for most foods that require an hour or longer to cook.

4. Keep oven door closed while cooking. Each time it is opened, heat escapes. Time what you cook instead of peeking.

5. When baking in a glass or ceramic utensil and the recipe specifies a metal utensil, lower the oven setting by 25 degrees (except for pastry). Glass and ceramics transfer heat better than metal.

5. Use retained oven heat to warm food and plates.

7. Don't use the oven as a room heater.

8.   Preheat broiler only for *rare* steaks.

9.   Use of an outdoor grill is an alternative to cooking indoors on your range. It doesn't increase energy consumption. And if your home is air conditioned, cooking outdoors on a grill helps ease the cooling load by keeping the cooking heat outdoors.

10.   Match pan size with corresponding size surface unit.

11.   Tight-fitting lids keep heat in utensils for faster cooking.

12.   Have all the family eat at the same time to avoid reheating meals for every member of the household. This saves extra work as well as energy.

13.   Start cooking vegetables on high heat and reduce to a lower setting once steam begins to escape.

14.   Cook foods at the lowest possible setting.

15.   Use the minimum amount of water for cooking. Don't lift cover or stir unnecessarily. This not only saves energy; it saves vitamins as well.

16.   Use a pressure cooker if possible; it cuts cooking time and energy use.

17.   Never leave surface units or oven on when not in use.

18.   Cook one-dish and oven meals.

Refrigerator

1.   Buy the size refrigerator that fits your specific needs. One that's too large wastes space and electricity.

2.   Set controls to maintain proper temperature. When set too low, energy is wasted.

3.   Don't overcrowd shelves or otherwise block free circulation of cold air.

4.   Before opening the door, know what you're looking for! Standing there with the door wide open costs money and energy. While cooking, plan trips to the refrigerator so several items may be retrieved at once.

5.   Frost acts as an insulator and makes it hard for the freezer compartment to remove heated air. Defrost as soon as frost becomes ¼ inch thick.

6.   Clean evaporator pan, condenser coils, fins, and motor

often. Dust that can accumulate in a short time blocks coils and decreases efficiency.

7.   Keep the kitchen cool. A 15-cubic-foot self-defrosting refrigerator will use 24 percent more energy when the room temperature is 90° F than when 70° F.

8.   Allow adequate wall and cabinet clearance. Giving the unit room to breathe helps hold costs down.

9.   Replace door gasket if it leaks cold air.

Freezer

1.   Place the freezer in a cool, dry, well-ventilated spot and defrost it at least once a year.

2.   The freezer should be kept full. This helps prevent loss of cold air when the door is opened. A half-empty freezer is a luxury to own and operate.

3.   Cool hot foods quickly. Package, label, and place in freezer immediately.

Small Appliances

1.   Usually small equipment, such as coffee pots, electric frying pans, and toasters, take less energy than large equipment.

2.   Use toaster rather than oven when it is feasible to do so.

3.   Use the electric coffee pot in place of the coffee pot over the range unit.

4.   Use the electric frying pan instead of a frying pan on range unit.

5.   Avoid operating small appliances in drafts; cool air can reduce their efficiency.

Lighting

1.   *Lighting consumes over 16 percent of all electricity used in American homes.* Turn off lights in unused rooms, especially in summer because light produces heat.

2.   Get the most out of the lights you do use. Dust bulbs frequently and keep fixtures clean.

3.   Use lower wattage bulbs.

Around the House and Yard

1. Turn the radio, TV, and stereo *off* when not in use.

2. Use *hand* tools—lawn mowers, pruners, and clippers—whenever possible.

3. Keep all appliances clean and in good working order.

4. Don't block intake vents on any appliance that requires air circulation.

5. Read the manufacturer's operating instructions and follow them carefully.

6. Don't heat your swimming pool in summer or all winter if it's kept covered and unused. It takes as much energy to heat as a small house does.

To make your own comparisons between kilowatt hour usage of different appliances, follow this simple procedure: (1) Read the name plate on the appliance to determine its operating wattage. (2) Estimate how many hours you might use the appliance in one month. (3) Multiply wattage by total hours to get watt hours of usage. (4) And divide by 1,000 to determine the kilowatt hours used.

11

SECURITY FEATURES

Years ago most crime occurred in the slums of large cities. If you lived in a "nice" neighborhood in the suburbs, you were relatively safe. Today it's different. Depressed areas still register a high rate of crime, but the "nice" suburban neighborhood is now a prime target for thieves since modern transportation can take them anywhere that prosperity has created a bonanza of things to steal. One need only to read the newspapers to find endless reports of burglaries in the suburbs. Touching on the absurd are true accounts of homes being stripped of their total possessions while neighbors watched! Worse yet are many heinous crimes committed against innocent victims in their homes during day and night while screams are heard but unheeded.

The false security associated with living in a nice neighborhood must be dispelled, and reality must be faced—there are amoral people waiting for the opportunity to harm you. Unpleasant as it is, this is a fact of twentieth-century American life. What is the solution?

You must be on the defensive and protect yourself and your property from those intent on harming you. If you place utmost value on your family, yourself, and your home, then you should plan carefully for the maximum possible security. Unfortunately, there is no absolute insurance against an intruder's getting into your home; this has been proven through the ages. You can build your home to resemble a medieval fortress with moat, stone wall, and booby traps, but there has been no fortress throughout history that was not eventually invaded and conquered by intent men.

What's the use to bother with any security measures at all if this is the hopeless situation? It's not hopeless, and you *can* protect yourself. The object is to place so many obstacles in the potential burglar's way that at least one of them will deter him from his intentions. Few burglars will battle obvious security measures, and then, knowing you have prepared for them, risk meeting further unknowns inside the house. The idea is to *deter* the potential burglar. If the professional knows your home contains some item he wants, he will plan his crime carefully and probably succeed. Most home burglaries, however, are not committed by experienced professionals but by amateurs and small-time crooks who break in and take whatever they happen to find. Your success will come by making the job too difficult and risky for this type of criminal who wants to make a fast, uncomplicated "hit" and be on his way.

The security features of your home constitute deterrents to the potential intruder. Your purpose is to discourage him from even trying to enter, and then if he does attempt to break in, he will find it too difficult and risky to chance going farther and will give up and go away. There are many mobile deterrents, such as weapons and security dogs, that you can bring into your home—but the best course to take is to build in as many systems as possible that are permanent, visible, and operating parts of the house. You want deterrents that will function under two conditions:

1. When you are at home (to protect your life as well as property)

2. When you are away and the house is empty

A major criterion to follow when choosing your deterrents is that they and their components be installed in ways and situated in places that would make their deactivation by burglars impossible. An elaborate electric alarm system serving all windows and doors is useless if the alarm bell is located in an accessible position. One clip of the wire to the bell could clear the way for easy entrance through any window or door. Security floodlights located so low to the ground that a person can reach up, unscrew the bulb, and plunge the area into darkness is no security at all.

Complex, sophisticated alarm systems can be extremely expensive, but locks and lights are two areas in which you can build in effective security features with little or no extra cost. When analyzing the needs to burglar-proof your home, you will find that *planning* is the key. Efficient deterrents can cost very little, if any, extra. For example, you must have locks on doors and windows. Don't settle for standard locks; select burglar-resistant ones. The difference in price is negligible, but one is useless and the other effective.

Locks

One of the most unnerving experiences we recall was when we were fumbling for our apartment key and realized we had locked ourselves out. A friendly repairman working next door saw our predicament and volunteered to help. He explained that he could open any door with a credit card and asked if we could produce one for him to use. Unbelieving, we handed him a card and presto!—our door was open! We thanked him, he returned to his work, and we resolved that when we built *our* home it would have locks requiring *our* key, not a credit card!

Doors do not come with locks already affixed. Your selection of locks is installed after doors are hung. Builders customarily use one or two lines of locks and will encourage you to select from what they usually put in their houses. Unfortunately, many of these are selected for their aesthetic qualities only, with no thought to whether they do anything more than hold the door closed, and subsequently they can be opened with a credit card. When discussing materials with your builder, demand locks that will lock! As with many items in your house, you can install first quality for very little extra expense. You must buy locks —add a dollar or two more per lock and get secure ones (and never let keys get out to workmen). Most people select a fine lock for the front door and may even purchase a *dead bolt* type that gives superior protection, but they usually fail to give the same consideration to all outside doors, especially the basement one that often opens in the back, is concealed by shrubs, and is poorly lighted or in total darkness.

Your house will have several outside doors—front, kitchen, basement, patio, and garage. Instead of selecting one type of lock for all doors, select locks specifically for each door as the uses of that door indicate. For example, if the basement door will never need to be unlocked from the outside, install a dead bolt lock that is bolted from the inside only, and consequently there will be no lock outside for an intruder to work on. The sliding glass patio door is similar. A dead bolt lock inside makes unauthorized entrance impossible. Also, some sliding doors can be lifted off their tracks and removed and thus require another locking device to prevent this. Lock manufacturers have displays in supply stores, and you may obtain catalogs that give details, styles, and prices. Collect several of these, study them, and plan a lock system for your house. It is quite possible that you will have a different type of lock on each outside door. All can be of the same artistic design, color, and materials if you wish, or they may be coordinated to the individual decor of each room.

A dead-bolt lock is the safest kind. It can be opened only with a key and cannot be jimmied with a credit card or knife.

The best locks are of no value if they are not used. What will you do when the front door bell rings? Will you unlock the door and find the caller is not the neighbor you thought was coming over? Or perhaps you expected a delivery man, and it turns out to be a psychopath after a victim. Several devices allow you to ascertain the identity of callers without negating your lock system. A peep-hole or "viewer" in the door gives you a wide view of the other side to see who is there without the visitor seeing you or even being aware that you are viewing him. This addition may cost only a dollar or two, and it may save your life. A chain lock permits the door to be opened a few inches, but it is useless against moderate pressure from the outside. A speak-through device is a security measure that allows you to converse with the caller without ever opening the door.

Unsecured garage doors invite thieves. Nothing is more convenient for a thief than having the protected garage area for working on the door to the inside. Your garage door needs a secure lock that you can lock from either outside or inside. In addition, place another good lock on the door leading from the garage into the house. A dead bolt type is recommended for this door.

When working on plans for your home, prepare a set of lock plans. Question the uses of each door in each room and decide what types of locks are needed. Follow the basic criterion of convenience and practicality of the system; if it is so complicated and complex it requires a staff to operate your system and hinders your mobility, you won't use it. In this case you might as well use standard "credit card locks" and hope for the best, but this need not be the situation. Plan carefully, and then enjoy the peace of mind a good lock system will give you.

Windows

"Burglars Welcomed" is the message windows frequently broadcast to those searching for a house to rob. To aid your burglar, locate ground level windows in unlighted, shadowed areas behind thick bushes. And of course, use standard bottom-of-the-line windows with their next-to-nothing locks to provide him easy access. Ridiculous? Not at all!

You can't locate all windows out of reach, nor can you forgo shrubs around the house, so what can be done to secure windows against unwanted entrance? A combination of measures can be taken. Double glazing or insulating glass automatically makes any cutting more complicated, and because the heavy glass is fit into frames, it cannot be removed by merely scraping off some putty. The standard double-hung window that slides up and down and the horizontal sliding window are less safe than casement, awning, hopper, or jalousie windows that are opened by an inside crank. The latter also do not present as large openings for entrance as do the double-hung and sliding types which usually provide areas large enough for a grown man to crawl through.

Locks on many windows are such that the slightest pressure on the outside portion of the window disengages the lock, rendering it completely useless. The old fashioned twist lock of the double-hung window is still commonly used and succumbs easily to outside tampering. Inside lever locks used on casement, awning, jalousie, and hopper windows cannot be sprung or opened from the outside without first breaking the glass. These types are among the best for safety.

Glass panels in kitchen, basement, and front doors invite trouble. Often these are held in place with putty or a strip of wood on the outside. Removal of one pane provides access to reach in and open the door from the inside. If you want a window in a door, locate it high and out of reach of the door lock.

Lights

Energy conservation should not curtail adequate security lighting. Light is one of the best deterrents—thieves do not want to be seen. Most of them want to get in, steal, and leave without an encounter. Providing adequate lighting in your home should not stop with providing illumination for the various activities in each room, but a special plan of security lighting should be developed during the planning stage, and this system should be built in during initial construction. Security lighting may be divided into three basic types:

1.   Inside lighting throughout the house

2.   General outside lighting

3.   Special outside security lighting

A home should not be cloaked in total darkness when the family retires at night. Not only is it convenient to have some light if one arises during the night, but a dimly lighted house is distasteful to an intruder. Of course, a lamp can be left on, but this often gives more light than is desired throughout the night. If your lights are controlled by dimmers, it's easy to leave certain areas softly lighted, or special small night lights can be built into the ceilings for this purpose.

Of immeasurable value are automatic electric timers that can be regulated to turn on and off certain house lights at preset times. This gives the effect that the house is occupied when the family is away for either short or extended periods. Based on the theory that burglars prefer not to have encounters with the occupants, this device can be quite effective. Automatic timers can also control outside lights.

You probably plan to have outside lights at the usual places—front door, back door, garage, and drive. Fine, but if you want them to provide security as well as light, don't waste your money on the standard kind that usually can be reached and deactivated in a matter of seconds. Recessed lights in frames requiring tools for opening can be situated in the soffit above the doors, and in most cases they can be reached only by a ladder. Unfortunately, there is no way to prevent intentional blackout of post lanterns; nevertheless, lights along the drive add to the general deterrence of intruders.

Special outside security lights can be very effective if properly installed. Plan this light phase so you can flood the entire outside of your house in bright light. If you are building a multistory dwelling, a dual unit can be placed under the roof at each corner, directing light on two sides. In recessed areas, additional lights should be directed into the dark shadows to prevent blind spots. Being elevated, these lights are out of reach and cannot be removed. They should be included in the general lighting diagrams, not added later with wires running up the outside of the house! These lights, like all others, are of no value if they can be extinguished from the outside. One switch to the security lights should be located in the master bedroom.

Alarm Systems

Electronic alarm systems for your home are available in three basic types: perimeter, light-sensitive, and wave systems. For greatest effectiveness, they should be planned and built in, although all can be added later. Costs range from a few hundred dollars into thousands depending on the complexity of the system and the difficulty of its installation. Some systems also require a monthly service fee.

A perimeter system protects the entire perimeter of your home by having each window and door wired with a switch that sounds an alarm if an intruder tries to enter. Perimeter systems can have batteries to continue operation during natural power failure or if the power lines are intentionally cut. You may choose from several kinds of warnings— loud horns, telephoned prerecorded messages to the police, radio transmitted messages, or alarms at a neighbor's home. Fire alarms and distress buttons (if you are attacked or injure yourself) can be added to the basic perimeter alarm system wiring.

Light-sensitive systems are useful for a single entrance or hallway, but they are not practical for the entire house. They work on the principle of an alarm being tripped when a beam of light is broken by an intruder's passing between the source of the light and the light-sensitive receiver.

Wave systems flood an area with microwaves, radar waves, or ultrasonic waves that are reflected by stationary objects. A moving object changes the wave pattern and sets off an alarm. Wave transmitters have limited range, and several are required to fill a house completely, making this type of system less practical for large homes.

When investigating specific alarm systems available in your area, ascertain the following:

1. How does the intruder trip the alarm?

2. How do *you* avoid tripping the alarm on entering and leaving your home?

3. How do you deactivate the system if it's accidentally tripped?

4. Can an intruder easily bypass the system?

5. What warnings are given?

6. What optional features are available, such as smoke, fire, and distress alarms?

7. Who will install the system? Is their integrity to be trusted?

8. What is the cost—initial, operating, and service?

No alarm system will give 100 percent security, but a good system, carefully planned and efficiently installed, can offer much protection. However, you must bear the responsibility to use it correctly and constantly. It will do nothing if you leave it turned off or if you throw the front door open in a burst of exuberance without first learning the identity of the caller.

Your home should provide security and peace for you at all times. You cannot enjoy this if the door is left open and you rely on romantic trust in your fellow man. Unfortunately, the only way you can feel the warmth, comfort, and protection of your "den" is by barring the outside world from entering. The more obstacles you place in the path of the potential intruder, the better chance you have of retaining your safety, property, and peace.

12

BUILD A HEALTHY ENVIRONMENT

Awareness of features of your house that can be helpful or harmful to your family's health is important and should be reflected in the design of your house and the selection of basic equipment and materials.

Some modern home plans call for fixed glass in all windows, correlated with an air conditioning system that makes opening windows for cool breezes unnecessary. Not only is this an extravagant use of power, but although the machine cools the house, it does not bring in a new supply of oxygen-rich air, nor does it exhaust the old stale air filled with impurities (unless it is one of the very few specifically equipped with a fresh-air intake). Just cooling and recirculating the same air is not enough, and such a system is completely useless during a power failure. Windows that never can be opened under any conditions should not be located throughout the entire house. Fixed glass is attractive and you may design some in, but plan your total ventilating system so that most rooms have at least one ventilating window and good cross-ventilation can be achieved if desired.

Air conditioning in torrid climates provides innumerable health benefits. Babies reared in air conditioned homes seldom have heat rashes. And air conditioning allows adults who suffer from excessive fatigue, irritability, and diseases caused by heat to perform their daily duties in optimum health even during hot weather. Air conditioning also inhibits growth of molds, mildews, and disease-carrying insects. Because the power consumed in the cooling process is great, air conditioning should be used judiciously—only when needed and just to the comfortable, not cold, point.

Winter colds can be reduced with humidity-controlled air. The humidifier is attached to the furnace and adds moisture to the air after it has been filtered and heated.

Two other environmental control devices—humidifiers and electronic air cleaners—can be installed in your home to provide further health benefits. Together they consume about as much power as your black-and-white television set. Electronic air cleaners are available as free-standing units and can be added as a piece of furniture at any time, in any room. The entire house can be filled with pure air, free of pollen, smoke, dust, and odors by installing a unit in your ducted system serving the furnace or air conditioner. This type of air cleaning system can be regulated to operate continuously by circulating air, or only when the furnace or air conditioning units are active. Such a system can keep your house over 90 percent free of airborne particles—a housekeeping boon as well as a health benefit.

Humidifiers can be purchased to maintain a desired moisture content in the air of your home. Like electronic air cleaners, these units also are available for individual rooms, or one master humidifier can operate through the ducted system in conjunction with the furnace or air conditioner. Many people experience great relief from respiratory disorders when they are able to control the humidity in their home.

It is essential to your family's health that your home be adequately heated. Don't try to cut corners on your heating system. This item is calculated in the total house price, and the additional cost for a first-rate system is relatively small. The heating system should be suited to your specific geographical area. What might be adequate to heat a 2,000-square-foot home in Florida could not give the same degree of comfort for a similar house in Maine. Your heating contractor, gas company, or electric company can compute your heat needs and suggest an appropriate system. If you plan a furnace, give consideration to its location for maximum utilization and minimum heat loss (discussed in Chapter 8). The type of system you choose should be determined by cost, effectiveness, energy efficiency, lasting quality, and cleanliness.

There must be a specific means for the removal of extra pollutants added to the air of your home. Nearly every kitchen today is equipped with a hood over the stove. Many of these merely draw air through charcoal filters to remove smoke particles but make no attempt to rid the area of steam, odors, and heat. If possible, plan your stove to be located along an outside wall to utilize an exhaust fan type of hood (vented directly to the outside), which will quickly remove smoke, heat, odors, and steam from the house. Exhaust fans are also excellent for ridding bathrooms of steam.

The open fireplace is another source of air pollution. This venerated landmark of early Americana has left the living room in most homes and is now in the family room or den. Its original purpose was to heat the house and cook the food. A few modern American homes in mild climates still use fireplaces as the sole sources of heat, and some families in areas subject to frequent power failures depend on their fireplace as an emergency stove. A fireplace, however, is usually added for atmosphere, and few things equal the comfort and feeling of well-being radiated by a blazing, popping fire on a cold winter night. But while you enjoy the cheeriness of your hearth, smoke is adding pollution to your home and neighborhood. Carefully evaluate a fireplace instead of automatically including it in your plans.

Give attention to flooring as related to the general health features of your home. Do you have children and pets? Their habits should be considered and planned for if you wish to live in a clean, sanitary home. The nursery floor might be pretty covered with a fluffy pastel carpet, but think of the many spills that occur there while baby is confined to the crib and later when he starts crawling! An easily washable surface of vinyl or poured plastic can be cleaned daily in a few minutes, and it won't harbor germs and hidden filth. Pets, likewise, have accidents, and if you are going to keep a pet in the house at all, plans should be made concerning its eating area, where its water will stay, and its bathroom facilities. Don't sacrifice all aesthetics and select your floors only for the practical aspects of children and pets, but if you're going to have them, provide realistically for their needs in order to maintain a healthy home.

A trash compactor helps keep the kitchen sanitary and tidy, and takes up little space if included in the initial planning.

A kitchen disposer and trash compactor (together using less power than your coffee pot) reduce kitchen garbage and help greatly in providing a healthy environment inside your house, but the storage of garbage outside until pickup day is a real and ever-present problem. The garbage can area should be included in your total plans and incorporated into your landscape scheme. If curbside pickup has been introduced as a cost-saving measure in your area, plan the location of your containers so that you can get them easily to the street on pickup days. Nothing is more incongruous to a beautifully conceived estate than a platoon of battered garbage cans in plain view. Tightly covered cans should be placed away from the house, firmly secured in an upright position safe from prowling scavengers, and concealed by fences, walls, or shrubs. Cans in the carport or garage are neither sanitary nor aesthetic.

Add another dimension to your family's well-being—build a healthy environment.

13

SAFETY FEATURES

Safety features pay off. They are neither showy nor luxurious, and you may never know if they work, but they may actually determine whether you recline in your Roman bath or a hospital bed, or successfully broil the steak or burn down the house. Safety features help ensure your family's well-being by eliminating the pain and emotional upheaval of accidents.

When planning the safety features of your home, each item presenting potential danger must be evaluated and weighed against its desirability. For example, stairs present the potential danger of falls, especially for the very young and the old; but a multistory house is desirable for energy and building economy, and you may simply prefer that style. Consider how much danger your family would be exposed to by stairs, whether it would be permanent or of temporary duration, and if the danger could be circumvented easily without changing styles. If you are young and in good health, your potential stair problems in old age should carry little weight. Or if you are concerned over your toddler's falling, you might solve that temporary situation with a gate at the top of the stairs. If, however, there is a member of your household for whom stairs would be a permanent hazard, the desirability of a multistory home would diminish.

You never know the usefulness of safety features built into your home if you never have an accident. You realize their value only if you don't have them and an accident happens. Many home accidents occur in kitchens, on stairs, and in bathrooms that are like booby traps set by the occupants. Look at potential trouble areas and remember where you and your family have had accidents. You will find that most accidents centered around the careless use of, and inadequate provisions for, the forces of *fire, electricity, water,* and *gravity.*

Fire

Many fires can be prevented by using common sense, such as not smoking in bed or disconnecting the coffee pot when leaving for a holiday, but what precautions can be built in?

Selection of fireproof or fire-resistant construction materials can lessen your chances of a serious fire. Asbestos, stone, brick, metal, and glass are nonflammable materials. Other materials, such as some plywood paneling, are treated to be fire resistant and are slow to ignite or burn, thus containing a fire long enough for you to discover it and do something about it. Roofing is available in various degrees of fire resistance and constitutes a major factor in your fire insurance rate—that with the least resistance to burning carries the highest premium. You cannot build your house entirely of nonflammable and fire-resistant materials, but by using them where you have a choice, you will diminish the possibility of a holocaust.

A fire extinguisher should always be located near the stove.

Where will you have open flames that could malfunction and ignite other areas? In fireplaces, furnaces, and gas appliances. Some building codes allow the flame types of furnaces to be located almost anywhere. They may be found in inaccessible attic areas, converted coat closets, and other places where a fire could be raging out of control before anyone would be aware of it, and then it could not be easily reached by firemen. Remember, building regulations are written to ensure minimum construction considered safe for habitation. Do you want this or more?

If you're going to have a fireplace, plan for it to contain the fire. Of course, you will have the usual screen to prevent large sparks and coals from popping out, but fluffy carpeting brought within twelve inches of a roaring fire is perilous because sparks can go over or under the standard screen. Build a wide hearth with a ridge to prevent coals and ashes rolling out. Glass screens are available to contain the fire, and you might investigate these. Above all, have at least one good fire extinguisher in your home. Attach it to the wall in an accessible place close to a danger area. Many home fires can be prevented with a little planning and precaution.

Electricity

Electric inventions have replaced many devices once dependent on fire. The gas iron has been replaced by the electric iron, but therein lies another potential danger when improperly handled. Clean and safe if correctly installed and used, electricity is one of the great discoveries of civilization, but it can burn down your home or cause your demise. Building codes usually are quite thorough concerning the wiring of homes, and they specify quality and type of materials used and their methods of installation. Only licensed electricians may be employed to do the wiring, and official inspectors must approve the job. It seems certain that your electrical system would be adequate and safe. However, live wires dangling in the walls (never connected to switches or outlets that were never installed) are not uncommon occurrences. Likewise, water pouring out of basement switch boxes from underground conduits containing electric wires causes doubt about the thoroughness of electricians and inspectors! Don't rely on workmen or inspectors entirely—inspect everything yourself and make sure the work is done well. Be sure every wire is connected to something and every switch and outlet is wired. Inspect wiring and outlets in below grade walls for ground water seepage. Count your switches and outlets before and after the walls are closed up to prevent some from being covered over and lost.

General placement of electrical wall outlets in each room is regulated by local building codes. Some require a minimum of one outlet every ten feet around a room. Regardless of this, be sure you have enough so that the use of extension cords can be avoided. Think again of the specific uses of each area. Outlets high up on the walls might be desirable in the nursery because toddlers like to poke bits of metal into holes and cut cords with scissors! Outside outlets should be located beside the front and back doors, in the patio and pool areas, and other places where electrical needs can be anticipated. These outlets always should be the special outside type, equipped with waterproof hinged covers.

A flooded basement is a common occurrence in areas subject to hurricanes and other extraordinary weather conditions. Sometimes abnormal weather isn't even necessary for basement flooding of an inch or more. Accompanying this may be electrical power failure requiring you to open the switch box, and where is the electrical center of a home usually located? On the basement wall. What could be more hazardous than wading and standing in water to work on the electrical switches during a storm! The switch box can be located anywhere, so put it in the pantry, kitchen, or rear foyer—not the basement.

Water

Your water system is the most trouble-free and safest system in the house. Plumbing, like electrical wiring, is governed by local codes and must be passed by inspectors. As with the electrical system, its installation should be carefully checked by you. Although the system can do you little physical harm, it can cause house damage if pipes are not properly fitted or if a break occurs. The main cutoff valve should be accessible so that if the need arises you can quickly and easily stop all water from entering the house. Likewise, cutoff valves to the dishwasher, washing machine, and all plumbing fixtures should be located in easily accessible places.

Safety features combined with fun features can make that twentieth-century luxury, the home swimming pool, a source of great delight. Proper supervision of children's swimming is the responsibility of parents, but what about the potential dangers of the deserted pool? To prevent accidents when you are not in attendance, you must make the pool inaccessible. Basic precautions should include complete enclosure of the pool area by a fence that cannot be crossed by small children. This, however, is of no value unless all gates are secured with key locks. If you have a house door opening out onto the pool deck, this also must be equipped with a lock that cannot be opened by children from the inside, or all other precautions are useless. Similarly, windows or any other means by which children can reach the pool must be secured. By taking a few simple safety precautions, your home pool can bring endless pleasure to everyone.

Place a window low to the floor in the child's room so he can see out easily without risking falls climbing on a chair.

Gravity

Bathrooms are notorious fall areas because of the reduced friction of wet surfaces. Tubs and showers should have secure hand grips capable of sustaining the weight of an adult. Select tubs with nonskid bottoms, and tile the shower floor with a rough-surfaced ceramic tile. Cover the bathroom floor with carpet or rough tile, too.

Small children live in a world of giants. Almost everything in the average home is built for adults, who to children are towering giants, sitting at giant tables, looking out windows above the children's line of vision, and doing everything above *their* heads. To function in this environment, children must always reach up or climb up on something. Consider the child's size and scale down his room. He should not have to endure endless falls from climbing on stools and chairs to reach his things. Build his bathroom cabinets below the basin, not above it beyond his reach. Lower his closet rod so he can remove and replace coat hangers at age three. The rod can be raised higher as he grows taller and his coats get longer. Build his bookcases and toy shelves at convenient levels, and don't place his windows at heights above his eye level. Some unfortunate children never see out of their bedroom windows until they reach ten or twelve!

One impressive feature of modern home design is the open, uncluttered, spacious feeling created by the two-story ceiling with open catwalks between balconies. Although such effects can be scintillating, they may test or tease the laws of gravity. For the benefit of small toddlers and yourself, make catwalks secure with railings that cannot be crawled between or easily fallen over. Of course, all stairways should have good, sturdy hand rails, and spiral stairs should have a protective rail around the top.

Doors that swing open down *into* the basement stairs are hazards for anyone using the door from either direction, and lighting of stairwells should be controlled by two switches placed so that lights can be turned on before entering the area from either direction.

Falls can occur outside the house on steps and stepping stones. Rough stones embedded in soil may be beautiful and compatible with your natural landscaping, but they also can wobble and cause an unsuspecting visitor to lose his footing. Steps that become excessively slick after a rain are also hazardous. Choose rough materials for secure footing and install hand rails if necessary.

Additional Features

If you have small children, other safety precautions should be made in your home design for their welfare. Install a secure lock in the cabinet where medicines are to be stored. Provide a locked cabinet in the kitchen and laundry for cleaning chemicals and one in the garage for garden chemicals. Although most building codes now require it, *be sure* all glass doors are safety glass, and install extra safety bars across the bottom if more protection is needed. All locks in a child's area should

All door locks to children's areas should be the type that in emergencies can be opened from the outside with a nail or other small household object.

be the kind that can be opened quickly from the outside if he accidentally locks himself in.

Built-in safety features in your home contribute to a happier environment and fuller life. Many require only your planning and add no extra cost. They constitute some of the extras that make your home special.

14

PLACEMENT OF
HOUSE ON LOT

Perfect plans! The garden merged into the dining room through great expanses of glass, and the master bedroom suite opened onto a sun deck offering privacy and relaxation. Every feature was distinctive, and the entire house, carefully conceived to meet the needs of its owners, was a success—on paper. But when it was built, the neighbor's garage and garbage cans merged into the dining room through great expanses of glass, and the master bedroom suite opened onto a sundeck offering a front-row seat at the neighborhood ball game. So the owners ate in the kitchen and bought a sun lamp.

They had chosen a good lot that was large, had no drainage problem, and was well suited to their home style and landscaping, but they had placed the house poorly on the lot, not using their land well. A compatible union of house and land (utilizing the full potential of both) will give maximum pleasure in exchange for your efforts in building.

Your builder's concern with placing your house will center around structural and functional details. He will not want to build a foundation in a boggy marsh, nor will he want to blast your basement from solid granite. He will need adequate space to bring equipment in and move it around and a sensible route for utility lines. Listen to him because he is an authority on this aspect of placing your house, and occasionally a lot will have only one possible site suitable for building.

Walk your land and learn every feature of it. What are the natural characteristics—trees, springs, rock outcroppings, and plants? Where does the sun rise and set, and how will its rays strike the house?

Will there be shade in summer or danger from ice-laden trees in winter? Do strong winds blow across your land?

Your lot has four characters. Which one did you see when you selected and bought it? Was it spring when everything is fresh and new, was it summer when even the most common weeds are beautiful, was it autumn with brightly colored leaves waving in the crisp breeze, or was it perhaps winter with its blanket of snow emphasizing graceful silhouettes of trees and shrubs? Each season presents a different face of nature, and you should imagine all the seasons before making final decisions concerning the relationship of your house to its land and adjoining areas. Summer foliage may cover an unsightly structure in the next yard, and winter snow may hide the fact that the ground is barren and lifeless.

Are you concerned that people see your home? Then it should be visible to as many as possible—preferably on a corner lot—although in making it a showplace you will surrender a great deal of privacy. Perhaps you care little what passersby see and instead want every aspect of your house and land to serve *your* physical and psychological needs. If this is your preference, you will need imagination and courage, but follow through; express your individuality by placing your house in a secluded spot offering little disturbance from the passing parade on the street.

Have a topographical survey made. The "topo" is a detailed survey of your lot, showing elevation changes at regular intervals (two feet is satisfactory). In addition, if you wish, all major trees, large outcroppings of rock, streams, springs, and other natural features will be indicated along with building lines, rights of way, and easements. The topo is like an aerial view of your lot and gives a visual picture with exact measurements of everything of consequence on it. Topos are made by general surveyors, and some charge by the hour and others by the job. Get several bids because the cost for the same job might vary as much as $200 to $600 with different firms. Only a person experienced in these matters should risk doing business with a firm that quotes an hourly rate.

After receiving your topo, you are ready to begin serious placement of the house on the lot. *Using the same footage scale as the topo,* cut out a paper house outline of roughly the dimensions you will build. Place your paper house on your topo and move it from front to back, from side to side, and turn it to every possible angle. To help with this examination, draw in the neighbors' houses on lots next to yours and all other features within view. Remember, this is the time to change your mind because once the foundation is poured, the house can never be moved again.

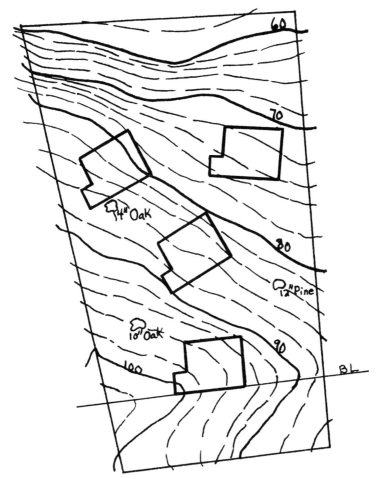

Move your house from front to back and from side to side, and turn it to every possible angle on the topo.

When you think you've found the correct location, stand in each imaginary room and look out each imaginary window.

- What will you see each season? Fences, streets, houses, garages, traffic lights, trees, meadows, and gardens?

- Do you look at your neighbors' houses? Into their windows? Or down onto their roofs?

- Will your neighbors look into your home?

- How much privacy can you have in your home?

- Is this the view and feeling you want?

- Will this location make the best possible use of your land?

When you've made your decision, carefully mark the ideal placement on your topo in pencil and on your lot with brightly colored streamers attached to wooden stakes. This will help your planner and builder greatly in their preliminary work with the project.

A large part of the total success of your home depends on its correct placement on your lot. You must know what you want from your house in relation to the land and total environment and then ensure getting it by carefully examining and questioning as suggested here. Make one final query: If placed at this location, at this angle, will the house and land give us all we want now and every day of the year? With careful forethought and planning it will.

15

LANDSCAPING

Most people leave trees and streams outside, but if you have these things on your lot and want them incorporated into your house (some individualists do), it must be known before any planning is begun and certainly before land alterations are made. Physically bringing nature into the house is not the customary way of enjoying ecology, but if you desire this, then there is much landscape designing to do before the house is begun. Even if you prefer the usual lawn, trees, and flowers to wild, intimate unions with nature, you should plan basic landscaping together with the placement of the house on the lot long before the first machine arrives. Too often landscaping is an afterthought, considered only when everything else is finished, and the homeowners spend the rest of their lives trying to reconstruct natural assets that fell early prey to bulldozers. They pay dearly for clearing, grading, and masonry that could have been done at little or no extra cost during building.

If you want to incorporate natural features of the land into the actual structure of your home, you must secure the services of both an expert landscape architect and an expert residential architect who have the knowledge, experience, and desire to undertake such an unorthodox task. Don't try to design that kind of thing yourself—it requires highly specialized skills. Nevertheless, if you wish to pursue such a route, study the features of your lot. Mark on your topo those features you wish to take advantage of, and use the topo as a starting point from which both landscape and residential architects can work, design, and plan together. Such a project can be exciting and challenging, and it brings a

Natural landscaping is the least expensive because it utilizes natural plants. The wild becomes controlled with the addition of carefully chosen ferns and statuary and selective removal of undesirable plants. (Photo by Matej Waschek)

feeling of great achievement and pleasure to all concerned. If you want it and can afford it, do it.

Modest landscaping is usually part of the total house-building project, and the builder plans on this work when he figures the cost of your home. He studies the lot and notes any required structures, such as retaining walls or bridges, that would add to the general landscaping budget. His bid will include these items along with a token number of shrubs and the standard lawn of your area. If you want more than the "builder's standard" you must, of course, expect to pay for it.

If you are not yet sure what you want in landscaping, the following items will help to stimulate ideas.

Look at Homes and Their Yards

Do you like what you see? Do you see specific items that you would want to look at forever, or do you have the feeling that even though something might be "cute" or unusual, you wouldn't want it permanently? Make lists of *desirable* and *undesirable* features. List those that you admire as well as those things that you perceive as obviously wrong. What type of lawns do you see? What kinds of plants?

What Style Do You Want?

Formal, casual, or natural? What style of house will you build? Landscaping should be compatible with house style. Conceive of the two together. Don't mix an Early American house with oriental gardens or New Orleans French architecture with natural landscaping!

Privacy or Togetherness?

Do you want the landscape to create a feeling and environment of seclusion and privacy, or do you want the open look so everyone can see you and you can see them?

Resale Value?

Contrary to what some real estate brokers say, landscaping *does* affect resale. The amount of money spent in the yard may not actually increase the dollar value of your home, but the *appearance* will affect its saleability. Attractive grounds cannot be ignored when a house is for sale. Many buyers make their final selection for no more valid reasons than a pretty little fish pool or a well-kept rose garden.

For You or Others?

Is the landscaping for others to see and be impressed, or is it for you? This is a major question seldom asked or given honest consideration. Ask it now and design what you really want.

Will It Work?

Don't fight the environment. Don't spend your life trying to force plants to grow where they aren't suited. Landscaping with palms and banana trees in Maine is not realistic. Don't waste time and money planting apple and birch in Florida. If you don't know what is naturally suited to your soil and climate, contact the specialists who do. State departments of agriculture, county extension agents (farm agents), and state forestry departments will be happy to provide you with scientific information concerning this.

Wall paneling lines parallel to trees, large areas of glass, and wood colors blend this home into the natural environment.

What Will It Cost?

Money

What will be the initial landscaping cost for trees, shrubs, walls, walks, flowers, lawn, grading, structures and so on? What will maintenance costs be for fertilizer, insecticides, water, equipment, seeds, mulches, and replacements? Maintenance often costs more than initial landscaping.

Personal Energy and Time

If you can afford an English gardener and staff, you can have any style of landscaping that is compatible with the environment. But if you have limited time and energy to spend on your yard, design your landscaping around one basic criterion—the amount of time and personal energy you want to devote to landscaping. After initial landscaping is completed, there is the eternal problem of care and maintenance. Mowing, trimming, mulching, pruning, fertilizing, raking, weeding, spraying, watering, reseeding, replanting, and endless other chores must be done continuously. How much of your life do you want to spend working in the yard? Do you prefer to spend vacations and weekends mowing or lounging? Competent yardmen are a thing of the past in many areas. Consider the value of your time and personal energy and decide how you want to use them.

Evaluate and weigh the involvement of different kinds of landscaping. If you want something personal and different from the "builder's standard," make long range plans, calling in a landscape architect if you need professional design advice. Long-range plans can easily be divided into stages to be developed over a period of years as your time and money allow. In the first stage take full advantage of the men and machines that will be working on your house by having planned clearing and grading done at building time. Later it could be difficult, even impossible, to get machinery in without tearing up fences, drives, and shrubs.

Discuss your landscaping with your builder and include in your contract (specifications section) exactly what landscaping he will do. Specify the clearing, grading, retaining walls, bridges, and plants he is to provide. If you have natural areas you want undisturbed, have a clear understanding that no materials are to be dumped there or utility trenches dug in the area.

When planning your landscaping, fully utilize the good qualities and features of the land, but be realistic—plan what you have time to maintain and money to water.

PART 2

GETTING DOWN
TO BUSINESS

16

FINANCING

Rare is the individual who can build without a mortgage. Most prospective homeowners must limit their desires to fit their finances. It is at this point that you must stop being emotional about your home and squarely face the hard, cold realities of money. Originality, innovativeness, methodical planning, daydreams, and work have gotten you to this point, but money, and only money, will get you any further.

Specific details of your loan will be determined by (1) state and federal laws in effect at the time, (2) the home-building market and general economy of your area, and (3) the individual regulations of the institution you do business with. Lenders in the same area must be competitive and their overall terms will be similar, but by shopping around you may find enough differences in their offers to make one institution definitely more attractive than another. You may seek money from the following kinds of institutions:

Lot Loans

- Commercial banks
- Mortgage companies
- Savings and loan associations

Home Loans

- Insurance companies

- Commercial banks

- Mortgage companies

- Savings and loan associations

LOT FINANCING

You can finance your lot almost as easily as you did your car. The one exception is that your attorney *must* draw up your contract, supervise all paperwork, and be present at the signing, *otherwise you may find you've bought it and someone else owns it!* Most lending institutions require a down payment of 20 percent to 30 percent and arrange monthly payments up to five years. These payments are comparable in amount to car payments, and many families have acquired their dream lot rather painlessly by substituting its payment for that of a new car. Your lot loan should be paid off before making a construction loan, and the money you have invested in your lot will count toward the down payment of the home loan.

HOME FINANCING

Three major types of loans are available on the new home market: VA, FHA, and conventional. Each has been created to fit a specific financial need, and a brief glimpse into the purpose of each and their basic differences should indicate which kind you need to investigate further.

VA (GI)

The VA loan is designed to help veterans get started again in the civilian world. It is administered through the Veterans Administration (VA), which supervises all appraisals, building regulations, and inspections. The government guarantees to the lender a sum of money not to exceed $17,500 to protect the lender against loss in case of foreclosure. VA loans are available for 100 percent of the cost of the house, with the upper limit dependent upon the individual's ability to repay the loan. Interest rates fluctuate with the market and federal regulations, but VA loans generally have the lowest interest rates of all loans. The lender makes up his loss of interest revenue by charging "points"—a sum of money based on the amount of the loan (one point equals 1 percent of the loan) and paid by the homeowner to the lender on a custom built home. Terms can be arranged up to 30 years. This type of loan is suited to the veteran who has no money for a down payment but who has sufficient income to meet monthly payments. It usually is used for a first home. Detailed information can be obtained from the Veterans Administration and your lender.

FHA

The FHA loan is administered by the Federal Housing Administration, and all homes built with such a loan must meet minimum property standards (MPS) set up by FHA. Down payments required are 3 percent of the first $25,000, 10 percent of the next $10,000, and 20 percent of any excess over $35,000. Maximum FHA loans are $45,000, and they are available for terms up to 30 years. Interest rates vary with the market and federal regulations, and FHA loans also carry a mortgage insurance premium of one-half of 1 percent of the outstanding balance. Lenders charge "points" on FHA loans when the interest rate is less than the prevailing rate on conventional loans.

If you will not need more than $45,000 to build your home, you might investigate an FHA loan through your lender or FHA office.

Conventional

You need money to make a conventional loan. Down payments vary from 15 percent to 30 percent of the total cost of the house and lot. Conventional loans are not guaranteed by the federal government, and the increased risk to the lender is reflected in higher interest rates and other conditions of the loan. Lack of government involvement enables the conventional loan to be sensitive to the general economy of the area, allowing lenders to be innovative in creating attractive loan packages to entice prospective customers while still reaping handsome dividends for their investors. Variations of the conventional loan adapted to the specialized needs of local communities have evolved throughout the nation. No VA or FHA inspection is made of conventionally financed housing, but many lenders insist that a house meet VA and FHA minimum requirements on the possibility that it might someday be resold on such a loan. Some lenders are lenient enough to allow you to borrow a limited portion of the down payment from another source if you can find one willing to lend it.

Terms of conventional loans vary according to the risk the lender takes. The best terms are available on a medium-priced house with a large down payment. As the percentage of down payment decreases, the interest rate increases. Likewise, as the house price rises into the upper brackets, the interest rate increases, simply because the lender has more of his money in one place. Private companies offer mortgage insurance to ensure the lender against loss in case of foreclosure (as the government does in the FHA loan), and if your down payment is small, you may be required to purchase this protection for the lender as well as pay a higher interest rate. Conventional loans are available for terms up to 30 years.

Lenders are interested in only one thing—*money*. Your house is no dream to them; it is merely an investment possibility, either good or bad. They will view you and your house against two standards: You will be measured against your ability to repay the loan, and your house will be measured against its resale potential in case of foreclosure. This may sound cold and harsh, but investors entrust their money to the good judgment of lending institutions, expecting a profit in return. If lenders became careless in their judgment, there soon would be no funds available for you to borrow.

A composite is made of your past history, present standing, and projected future financial status to determine your ability to repay the loan. The manner in which you handled previous obligations shows your feeling of responsibility toward debt. Your drive and perseverance under hardships in your job, in establishing your business, or in pursuing graduate degrees indicate desirable strength of character. Assets accumulated over the years reflect your thrift. Your present and predicted future income will be considered along with current debts and anticipated expenses. Family size and the ages of the members of your family will have a bearing on these factors.

Judgment of your ability to repay the loan will be partially subjective, depending on how you strike the person with whom you talk. You will be dealing with the most conservative part of the business establishment, and this will be no time to try to prove a point no matter how strongly you feel on current controversial issues. Women's apparel should be as discreet as an Altar Guild member's—hat, gloves, hose, heels, and a skirt of proper length. Men should be attired in suits, dress shirts, and ties of temperate color and design. It is understandable that you may be nervous or frightened, but arrogance, hostility, and tears will get you nowhere. Organize your thinking, make notes, and be businesslike in discussions. If you must take a child along, make him behave.

You will impress the lender with your attitude toward your home, so be enthusiastic and ebullient even though you know he will be totally serious.

What is the most popular home style in your area—the one you see stamped out over and over in every new subdivision that opens? Is it a three-bedroom split, with two and a half baths, fireplace in the family room, and sliding glass door onto the patio? Maybe it's a rustic ranch with a shake roof, or a Colonial, or California modern, or a Cape Cod. Whatever happens to be the popular house style in your area is the standard that the lender will use to evaluate your home to determine its resale potential. His money is safest in the house that will sell, and sell quickly, if it is ever placed on the market. The more your home differs from the popular one, the less attractive it is to the lender. This does not mean he will refuse to finance it if all other factors are favorable, but in the words of an experienced loan officer, "Go ahead and build what you want, but if it's different, you'll have to pay for it in higher interest rates, higher down payment, and shorter terms." If your house is similar to the popular house, its resale value will be good, entitling you to a more attractive loan proposal.

Your choice of builder will affect your chances of getting a loan. Lending institutions sadly know the difference between a good builder and a bad one. They know, too well, who will throw shoddy materials together and hide sorry workmanship under putty and paint. Their legal departments can name builders who leave town with construction funds in their pockets, leaving houses unfinished. Loan money is not secure in the hands of such people, and lenders will not be anxious to risk their funds. Ethics will prevent their outright recommendation or criticism of your builder. Nevertheless, you certainly can sense their attitude in your discussions. As one loan officer said, "No, ethics won't permit us to recommend your builder, but let me state this, the association would never hesitate to finance a home he builds."

You will defeat your purpose if you try to save money by acting as your own contractor or craftsman unless you have proven, professional experience. The total quality of a house influences its finished value, and lending institutions will not want to risk investing in the chance that you *might succeed* in an unfamiliar field. Without previous professional building experience, you could permanently impair the quality of your home, and lenders will not want to take the risk of supporting your inexperience.

It will take at least three trips to the lender to guide you successfully through the financing phase of your project.

Please do not leave any
questions unanswered

FINANCIAL STATEMENT

CONFIDENTIAL

DECATUR FEDERAL SAVINGS AND LOAN ASSOCIATION
Decatur, Georgia

Name_____ Address_____

For the purpose of procuring and maintaining credit from time to time in any form whatsoever, with the above named, for claims and demands against the undersigned, the undersigned submits the following as being a true and accurate statement of his financial conditions on the following date, and agree that if any change occurs that materially reduces the means or ability of the undersigned to pay all claims or demands against him, the undersigned will immediately and without delay notify the above named and unless the above named is so notified it may continue to rely upon the statement herein given as a true and accurate statement of the financial condition of the undersigned as of the close of business.

(Month)_____ (Day)_____ 19_____

ASSETS				LIABILITIES			
Cash on hand and in Banks*				Notes payable to Banks-Secured			
U. S. Govt. Securities - see schedule				Notes payable to Banks-Unsecured			
Listed Securities - see schedule				Notes payable to relatives			
Unlisted Securities - see schedule				Notes payable to others			
Accounts and Notes Receivable				Accounts and Bills due			
Real Estate Owned - see schedule				Unpaid Income Tax			
Real Estate Mortgages Receivable				Other unpaid taxes and interest			
Automobiles				Real Estate Mortgages			
Cash Value - Life Insurance				Payable - see schedule			
Household Furnish. & Personal Prop.				Chattel Mortgages and other			
Other Assets - itemize				Liens Payable			
				TOTAL LIABILITIES			
				NET WORTH			
TOTAL ASSETS				TOTAL LIAB. & NET WORTH			

SOURCES OF INCOME		PERSONAL INFORMATION	
Salary	$	Business or occupation	Age
Bonus and Commissions	$	Partner or Officer in any other	
Dividends	$	venture	
Real Estate Income	$	Married (wife's age) Children (ages)	
Other income - itemize	$	Single Dependents	
TOTAL	$		

GENERAL INFORMATION

Are you defendant in any suits or legal action?

Have you ever taken bankruptcy?
Explain:

*BANK RELATIONS – – – CASH ACCOUNTS	Checking	Savings	Amt. Pledged
NAME AND LOCATION OF BANK OR SAVINGS AND LOAN (show amounts pledged)			

(COMPLETE SCHEDULES ON REVERSE SIDE)

SCHEDULE OF U. S. GOVERNMENTS, STOCKS AND BONDS OWNED

No. of Shares or Face value (bonds)	Description	In Name of	Market Value

SCHEDULE OF REAL ESTATE MORTGAGES RECEIVABLE

Description of Property Covered	Date of Acquisition	In Name of	Amount	Maturity

SCHEDULE OF REAL ESTATE OWNED

Description of property and Improvements	Date Acquired	Title in Name of	Cost	Market Value	Mortgage	
					Amount	Maturity

SCHEDULE OF LIFE INSURANCE CARRIED, INCL. N.S.L.I. AND GROUP INSURANCE

Amount	Name of Company	Beneficiary	Cash Surrender Value	Loans

GIVE NAMES OF BANKS OR FINANCIAL INSTITUTIONS WHERE CREDIT HAS BEEN OBTAINED

Name	Date	High Credit	Basis

The undersigned certifies that both sides hereof and the information inserted therein has been carefully read and is true and correct.

_____19_____

Date Signed

Signature

L. 48-RIPCO

First Trip

Your first trip must be made before you talk with anyone about drawing your plans. You must know the price range you can comfortably afford because it would be folly to pay for plans for a $100,000 house if your ultimate limit is $60,000. The first question either a designer or architect must ask is, "How much money can you spend?" If your answer is evasive or uninformed, the results will inevitably be tragic. The lender can give you basic rules of thumb on what he feels you can afford, such as a mortgage two and a half times your gross annual income, or your total housing cost (payment, taxes, insurance, and utilities) not to exceed one fourth your gross monthly income. (See Appendix 1 for an estimate of your home-building power.) Discuss interest rates, number of years for repayment, and amount of down payment with him. Determine if you have enough down payment and what to do if you don't. Ask, also, how much cash you will need for escrow accounts, insurance, attorney's fees, surveys, and closing costs. Find out the general procedure in applying for and receiving a loan. Will it be made as a construction-permanent loan? If so, what payments must you make during construction, and when do your full payments begin? (Can the builder complete the house in that length of time?) Your lender can answer all these questions and give you a general idea of how he views your loan chances. But he cannot and will not commit himself until you have detailed plans and a signed building contract because both the house and the builder are factors in your loan.

Financing a home to be built differs from most other financing in that the item to be financed does not yet exist. The lender has only the written promise of a building contract, a set of plans, and the reputation of the builder by which he can evaluate the future finished home. Because the building contract *must* be signed before applying for a loan, the contract should allow for the chance that the loan will fall through [see page 193, paragraph 7(b)]. However, if you follow closely the procedures set forth in Part 2 of this book, there is little chance for failure.

Second Trip

Your second trip to the lender is a precautionary one. It is made after you and your builder have thoroughly examined and corrected your preliminary plans and the builder has given you a firm price. Make this trip before you have final plans drawn or sign a building contract. Ask the lender to examine your corrected plans, your builder, his price, and your financial status for anything that might hinder your chances of a loan. *Pay careful heed to what he says.* No contracts are yet signed, so it's not too late to make changes.

Third Trip

The third and last trip as a prospective customer is to make the formal loan application. You will need a set of your final plans and a signed building contract that your attorney has drawn up. Be prepared, also, to answer detailed financial questions, such as the ones contained in the form on pages 144–145. In a few days you will receive written notice of the decision. If it's positive, you will be given an offer that you must sign as indication of your acceptance.

If, however, you are turned down for your loan, the institution should explain why. The deficiency may be minor, allowing you to correct it easily and to reapply to the same institution. Should the deficiency be one you can't correct, your best hope for a loan would be to apply to a different institution, and better still, to a different kind of institution. Once you have accepted a satisfactory loan offer, building will commence within a few days.

17

GETTING YOUR PLANS

The importance of good plans cannot be overemphasized because it is impossible to get a good house from bad plans. Don't try to build your dream home from "kitchen table" plans—those drawn by a friend after taking a short drafting course at night school. Moreover, don't expect that talented young school of architecture undergraduate to produce buildable plans either. The person who draws your plans should have successful experience, detailed knowledge of the home-building industry, and many satisfied homeowners living in homes of his design. He should know the stock items found in any lumber yard and use them to the fullest extent with no waste. Your planner should be willing to let the needs of your family, not aesthetics, decree the design of your home. He should look upon the design project as your home, not his personal monument sculptured of brick and wood. Your plans are the crystallization of your ideas into directions to your builder and workmen. They are the mold in which your home will be cast, and they must be right. How can you distinguish good plans from bad ones? It's very simple! Good plans are:

- *Your ideas*—converted to blue and white
- *Buildable*—easily followed by local workmen
- *Affordable*—both plans and house

Professionally drawn plans are available from three sources: architects, residence designers, and publishers of ready-made plans.

Each has its own distinct advantages; evaluate all three in relation to your situation and select your best source. Before signing a design contract, consult your attorney if it involves more money than you can afford to lose!

Architect

"You must give me *unlimited funds* or unlimited design freedom, and even with the latter I can make no guarantees that the plans can be built within your budget, or even built at all" is a statement you may hear from an architect! Although he will contract to draw a set of plans for you, an architect will make no guarantee that the plans can be built within your budget, or even built at all. If you ask him to work within a restricted budget, he will often demand unlimited design freedom, dismissing all *your* ideas. Or if you have firm ideas about your house and appeal to him to work along these lines, he may request unlimited funds for the projected building cost. Few architects limit their businesses to houses. Most also design civic, commercial, and industrial buildings and may not be anxious to take on a less profitable house-designing job.

Architects make no commitments about the price of a house or the buildability of their plans. They justify this by saying they have no control over the building industry and therefore no control over the price put on a house. They work only with estimated costs and hope to be fairly current on the materials and labor market. Professional ethics prevent any direct association with the construction industry, so their tables of costs are remote from the everyday hassle of building and come to them in distilled, refined forms.

Aloofness from the noise of hammers and nails allows architects to think creatively, often intuitively spearheading desperately needed new trends in housing. But this same characteristic keeps them out of touch with the limitations of local workmen, a factor as restrictive as finances on the final realization of your home.

Popular magazines contribute to the misconception that you walk into the achitect's office bubbling over with enthusiasm about your house and lot, and he rushes to seize the opportunity of your great challenge to design a house costing $10 per foot (when the going rate is $25) just to show the world it can be done and to establish his name forever among the greats. The magazines never mention fees, leaving you with the comfortable feeling that reflected glory and satisfaction with a job well done are all the architect expects in return for his highly skilled, professional services. What a disservice to both architect and client to feature these one-in-a-million cases as though they were usual!

Examination of the architect's contract will probably show 10 percent of the building cost to be the basic fee for his services. To this may be added additional fees at comparable rates for other services he deems necessary, including that of professional consultants engaged during the project. Remember that the architect cannot guarantee the cost of the house, and you immediately realize that neither can he guarantee the amount of his fee when it is based on the cost of the house. His fee is *in addition to* the building cost. Therefore, if your house costs $60,000 to build, the architect's basic fee is $6,000, making a total of $66,000, excluding land.

What do you get for that $6,000? Essentially, *plans* (of which he retains ownership) and *observation* of the construction during which he makes every effort to protect the owner from defects and poor workmanship. But he assumes no responsibility for how the work is done, or even if it is done. His contract is complex, and your attorney *must* examine it carefully and advise you thoroughly on its full meaning.

Architects would soon starve if they could give you no more than their contract states. The real advantages of hiring one are subjective and intangible. Architects can draw creative, aesthetic, innovative new styles or detailed authentic reproductions of previous styles. There is definitely status connected to working with an architect, especially a recognized one. And he can be a real aid in observing the construction if your time is limited or if you simply feel that job is too big to undertake.

Residence Designer

A residence designer is a professional whose entire business is designing homes. Many do two kinds of plans: custom plans and stock designs presented in catalogs. Builders often use designers' stock plans for their speculation houses because the plans are both buildable and affordable. A builder's livelihood depends on the ease with which his men can follow the plans they are using. Time and materials are money to him, and he can't waste either trying in vain to make something work that was poorly designed. By limiting his business to single-family residences and keeping in daily close touch with builders, the residence designer has a concentrated in-depth knowledge of home building. His finger is on the pulse of the industry daily. This up-to-the-minute knowledge of local conditions, costs, labor, and availability of materials is the most important asset any planner can present you. The residence designer is no dreamer; he must be a realist and 100 percent practical. He speaks concretely about abstract ideas, giving you workable solutions to design problems. He works with aesthetics to the point of being pleasing, but he does not let aesthetics dictate the house.

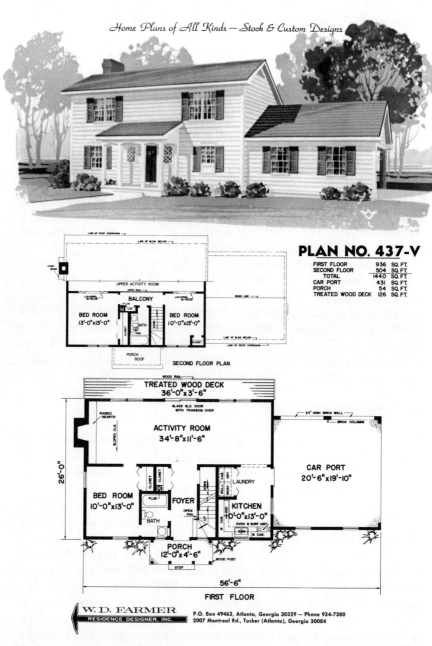

PLAN NO. 437-V

FIRST FLOOR	936	SQ. FT.
SECOND FLOOR	504	SQ. FT.
TOTAL	1440	SQ. FT.
CAR PORT	431	SQ. FT.
PORCH	54	SQ. FT.
TREATED WOOD DECK	126	SQ. FT.

SECOND FLOOR PLAN

UPPER ACTIVITY ROOM

BALCONY

BED ROOM
13'-0"x13'-0"

BED ROOM
10'-0"x13'-0"

BATH

PORCH ROOF

TREATED WOOD DECK
36'-0"x3'-6"

ACTIVITY ROOM
34'-8"x11'-6"

CAR PORT
20'-6"x19'-10"

BED ROOM
10'-0"x13'-0"

FOYER

KITCHEN
10'-0"x13'-0"

LAUNDRY

BATH

PORCH
12'-0"x4'-6"

26'-0"

56'-6"

FIRST FLOOR

W. D. FARMER RESIDENCE DESIGNER, INC.
P.O. Box 49463, Atlanta, Georgia 30329 — Phone 934-7380
2007 Montreal Rd., Tucker (Atlanta), Georgia 30084

Ready-made plans (stock plans) are available from many sources. You may get them from residence designers through their catalogs, by mail order from building magazines, and from catalogs sold in bookstores and at newsstands.

152

Take him your ideas and discuss them frankly, asking his advice and suggestions. Give him your budget limits and explain any other restrictions or limitations. Your family's needs are his prime concern, and he will work realistically within your budget to meet them. How much will he charge, and what do you get for your money? He may charge as little as $500 to custom design your $60,000 house. For that fee you get buildable, affordable plans, custom designed to *your* individual ideas. He, like the architect, retains ownership of the design. How do you find a residence designer? Look in the yellow pages of your phone book under *designer, draftsmen, residence designer,* or *home plan service*. Also call the local chapter of the National Association of Home Builders, which is always a good source of names of reputable people in the building industry. However, builders in your area are the principal source of names of good residence designers; ask them whose plans they use with confidence.

Ready-made Plans (Stock Plans)

Ready-made plans are available from many sources. You may get them from residence designers through their catalogs, by mail order from building magazines, and from catalogs sold in bookstores and newsstands. They are a bargain, often costing less than $75 for several copies of complete working drawings and a materials list that helps the builder determine costs. Ready-made plans are ideal for the cost-conscious homeowner and a great service to people in remote areas too far to commute to an architect's or designer's office. Designed by skilled professionals, ready-made plans represent more thought and refinement than some custom plans. With thousands to choose from (in all possible styles and suitable to all types of terrain), you likely can find a close representation of your ideas. Then, using one or more of the following methods, you can customize ready-made plans to your individual needs.

1. *A different elevation* can change the style of a house without disturbing the interior. The same basic plan can become Mediterranean, Contemporary, or Colonial by changing exterior finishing materials, window design, and trim details. Many ready-made plans have more than one suggested elevation included, and you and your builder can design others.

2. *Expand a small floor plan,* making all rooms larger by moving the exterior walls out the desired number of feet.

3. *Add extra rooms* to the existing plan to achieve the number and kind of rooms you need.

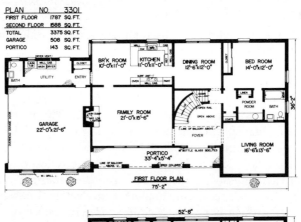

PLAN NO. 3301
FIRST FLOOR 1787 SQ. FT.
SECOND FLOOR 1588 SQ. FT.
TOTAL 3375 SQ. FT.
GARAGE 508 SQ. FT.
PORTICO 143 SQ. FT.

FIRST FLOOR PLAN
75'-2"

SECOND FLOOR PLAN

A different elevation can change the style of a house without disturbing the interior. (Courtesy of W. D. Farmer, Residence Designer, Inc.)

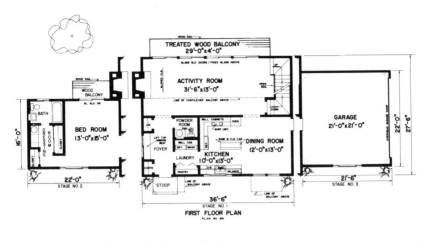

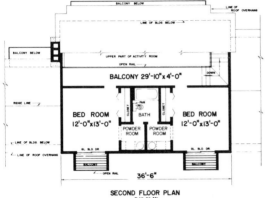

PLAN NO. 851

STAGE NO.1 - FIRST FL.	1004 SQ. FT.
SECOND FL.	511 SQ. FT.
TOTAL	1515 SQ. FT.
STAGE NO.2-FIRST FL.	352 SQ. FT.
TOTAL	1867 SQ. FT.
STAGE NO.3 - GARAGE	473 SQ. FT.
FINISHED BASEMENT	510 SQ. FT.

Add extra rooms to a plan you like to achieve the number and kind of rooms you need. A bedroom, dressing room, and bath were added to this plan on one side, and a garage was added on the other. (Courtesy of W. D. Farmer, Residence Designer, Inc.)

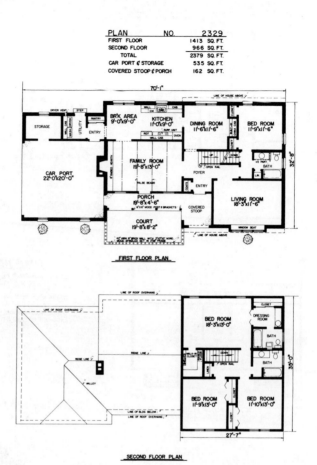

PLAN   NO.   2329

FIRST FLOOR	1413 SQ. FT.
SECOND FLOOR	966 SQ. FT.
TOTAL	2379 SQ. FT.
CAR PORT & STORAGE	535 SQ. FT.
COVERED STOOP & PORCH	162 SQ. FT.

Expand a small floor plan by moving the exterior walls out the desired number of feet, as in this plan (left) which grew from 2,379 square feet to

4. *Move interior walls* to rearrange the placement of rooms, closets, and halls, as well as to change the size of individual areas.

5. *Reverse the plan,* giving a mirror image to enable it to fit your land better.

6. *Move projections,* such as garage, deck, or rooms, to another location on the plan to realize better aesthetic balance or to make the plan more suitable for your lot.

7. *Convert garage, basement, and storage areas* into needed rooms, remembering to add more storage and garage space elsewhere if needed.

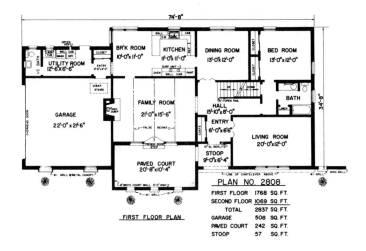

FIRST FLOOR PLAN

PLAN NO. 2808

FIRST FLOOR   1768 SQ. FT.
SECOND FLOOR   1069 SQ. FT.
     TOTAL   2837 SQ. FT.
GARAGE   508 SQ. FT.
PAVED COURT   242 SQ. FT.
STOOP   57 SQ. FT.

SECOND FLOOR PLAN

2,837 square feet (right). (Courtesy of W. D. Farmer, Residence Designer, Inc.)

It takes a great deal of effort on your part to select and customize a ready-made plan, and if you're not prepared to shoulder this responsibility, you certainly should have custom plans drawn. Any plans you order should be examined by your builder for conformance to local building codes. He can advise you on changes of design or floor plans and on the suitability of the plans to your lot. You can get a rough estimate of building costs by multiplying the square footage of the plan by the building cost per foot prevailing in your area. Add to this the cost of mechanical equipment and extra items such as prefab fireplaces and insulating glass. Thus, with skill and perseverance you can customize ready-made plans into just what you want.

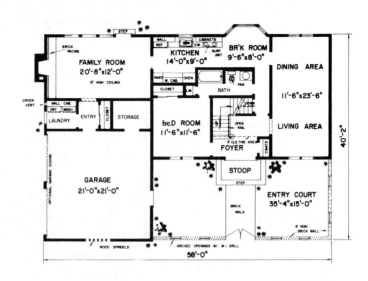

FAMILY ROOM
20'-8"x12'-0"
12' HIGH CEILING

BRICK FACING

STEP

WALL REF

KITCHEN
14'-0"x9'-0"

CABINETS
D.W.
SURF UNIT

BR'K ROOM
9'-6"x8'-0"

DINING AREA
11'-6"x23'-6"

PANT
W. CAB.
OVEN

CLOSET

LIN

BATH

FAN

LIVING AREA

DRYER VENT

WALL CAB.
DRY WASH

LAUNDRY

ENTRY

CLOSET

STORAGE

BED ROOM
11'-6"x11'-6"

DOWN

OPEN RAIL

FOYER

IF CLG THIS AREA

COATS

GARAGE
21'-0"x21'-0"

STOOP

STEP

ENTRY COURT
35'-4"x15'-0"

BRICK WALK

6' HIGH BRICK WALL

OPTIONAL GARAGE DOORS

WOOD SPINDELS

ARCHED OPENINGS W/ W.I. GRILL

58'-0"

40'-2"

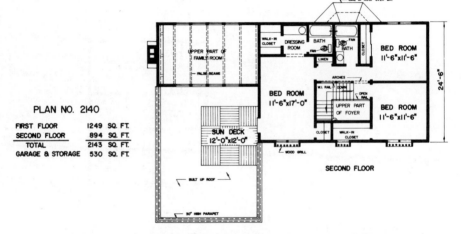

LINE OF ROOF OVER BAY

UPPER PART OF FAMILY ROOM

FALSE BEAMS

WALK-IN CLOSET

DRESSING ROOM

BATH

FAN

FAN

BATH

LINEN

CLOSET

BED ROOM
11'-6"x11'-6"

BED ROOM
11'-6"x17'-0"

W.I. RAIL

ARCHES

DOWN

OPEN RAIL

UPPER PART OF FOYER

CLOSET

WALK-IN CLOSET

BED ROOM
11'-6"x11'-6"

SUN DECK
12'-0"x12'-0"

WOOD GRILL

24'-6"

BUILT UP ROOF

30" HIGH PARAPET

SECOND FLOOR

PLAN NO. 2140

FIRST FLOOR	1249 SQ. FT.
SECOND FLOOR	894 SQ. FT.
TOTAL	2143 SQ. FT.
GARAGE & STORAGE	530 SQ. FT.

Projections, such as the family room and garage in these plans, can be moved to realize better aesthetic balance or to make the plan more suit-

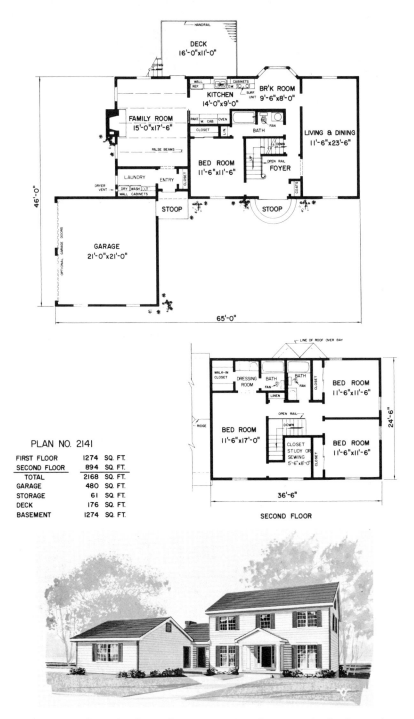

DECK
16'-0"x11'-0"

HANDRAIL

DOWN

KITCHEN
14'-0"x9'-0"

WALL
REF

CABINETS
D.W.

SURF
UNIT

BR'K ROOM
9'-6"x8'-0"

FAMILY ROOM
15'-0"x17'-6"

PANT. W. CAB | OVEN

CLOSET

LIN

BATH

FAN

LIVING & DINING
11'-6"x23'-6"

FALSE BEAMS

BED ROOM
11'-6"x11'-6"

DOWN

OPEN RAIL

FOYER

LAUNDRY

DRYER
VENT

DRY WASH LT
WALL CABINETS

ENTRY

CLOSET

COATS

46'-0"

STOOP

STOOP

GARAGE
21'-0"x21'-0"

OPTIONAL GARAGE DOORS

65'-0"

LINE OF ROOF OVER BAY

WALK-IN
CLOSET

DRESSING
ROOM

BATH
FAN

BATH
FAN

CLOSET

BED ROOM
11'-6"x11'-6"

LINEN

RIDGE

BED ROOM
11'-6"x17'-0"

OPEN RAIL

DOWN

CLOSET
STUDY OR
SEWING
5'-6"x8'-0"

CLOSET

BED ROOM
11'-6"x11'-6"

24'-6"

36'-6"

SECOND FLOOR

PLAN NO. 2141

FIRST FLOOR	1274	SQ. FT.
SECOND FLOOR	894	SQ. FT.
TOTAL	2168	SQ. FT.
GARAGE	480	SQ. FT.
STORAGE	61	SQ. FT.
DECK	176	SQ. FT.
BASEMENT	1274	SQ. FT.

*able for your lot. The basic house remains the same in both versions.
(Courtesy of W. D. Farmer, Residence Designer, Inc.)*

159

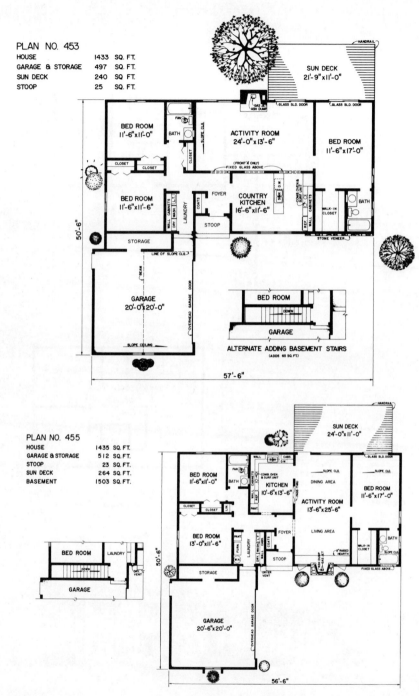

PLAN NO. 453

HOUSE	1433	SQ. FT.
GARAGE & STORAGE	497	SQ. FT.
SUN DECK	240	SQ FT.
STOOP	25	SQ. FT.

SUN DECK
21'-9" x 11'-0"

BED ROOM
11'-6" x 11'-0"

BATH

ACTIVITY ROOM
24'-0" x 13'-6"

BED ROOM
11'-6" x 17'-0"

CLOSET

CLOSET

FIXED GLASS ABOVE
(FRONT 'A' ONLY)

BED ROOM
11'-6" x 11'-6"

LAUNDRY

FOYER

COUNTRY
KITCHEN
16'-6" x 11'-6"

WALK-IN
CLOSET

BATH

COATS

STOOP

STORAGE

STONE VENEER

LINE OF SLOPE CLG.

GARAGE
20'-0" x 20'-0"

BED ROOM

GARAGE

SLOPE CEILING

ALTERNATE ADDING BASEMENT STAIRS
(ADDS 65 SQ.FT.)

50'-6"

57'-6"

PLAN NO. 455

HOUSE	1435 SQ. FT.
GARAGE & STORAGE	512 SQ. FT.
STOOP	23 SQ. FT.
SUN DECK	264 SQ. FT.
BASEMENT	1503 SQ. FT.

SUN DECK
24'-0" x 11'-0"

HANDRAIL

BED ROOM
11'-6" x 11'-0"

BATH

KITCHEN
10'-6" x 13'-6"

DINING AREA

BED ROOM
11'-6" x 17'-0"

CLOSET

ACTIVITY ROOM
13'-6" x 25'-6"

LIVING AREA

BED ROOM
13'-0" x 11'-6"

LAUNDRY

FOYER

WALK-IN
CLOSET

BATH

STOOP

STORAGE

BED ROOM

LAUNDRY

DOWN

GARAGE

GARAGE
20'-6" x 20'-0"

50'-6"

56'-6"

Moving interior walls rearranges the placement of the kitchen and activity room and changes the size of the front bedroom in this plan. (Courtesy of W. D. Farmer, Residence Designer, Inc.)

PLAN NO. 360 S.F.

UPPER LEVEL	1305	SQ. FT.
LOWER LEVEL (FUTURE FINISHED)	657	SQ. FT.
GARAGE & STORAGE	631	SQ. FT.
STOOP	26	SQ. FT.

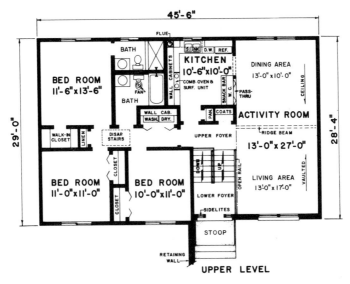

UPPER LEVEL

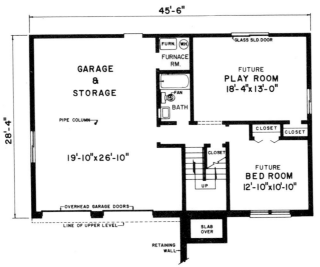

LOWER LEVEL

If needed, part of the basement of this plan can be converted into a play-room and bedroom. Should more room be desired, the garage and storage area could also be converted into rooms and a carport added outside. (Courtesy of W. D. Farmer, Residence Designer, Inc.)

18

SELECTING YOUR BUILDER

After you have secured your lot, made your first trip to your lender, and completed your preliminary house plans, you are ready to take another major step toward the realization of your home—selecting your builder. An extraordinary design and even an unlimited budget do not mean the house will be erected as indicated or even that it will be erected at all, if you don't have the right builder.

You must have complete trust and confidence in your builder's ability and ethics, otherwise the relationship cannot succeed. There are many areas in which the builder must use his own judgment and deviate from customary procedure to achieve the desired result, and it is here that you must trust him explicitly. What then, must you look for in a builder, and how do you go about finding him? There are many things to investigate and learn about a builder before signing a contract with him. Review the following suggestions and be sure you're aware of every aspect concerning the builder you select.

You probably looked at many houses under construction when you were getting ideas for yours, but from what point of view were you looking—space, style, design, colors, attractiveness? How carefully did you examine the quality of lumber used for joists or how tightly the subfloor fit? Did you notice the width of the footing or the material of the sewer pipes? Probably not, because that built-in oven and attractive living room carpeting caught your eye. The fun is over now, and it's time to get out the magnifying glass and play Sherlock Holmes. You will not win friends, but you may prevent ulcers while getting your home built.

Go house looking with a pen and notebook. When the salesman offers the grand tour, take it, but linger after he leaves and look in the corners, attic, basement, and all the secret places. Make notes under two headings: *Good Things* and *Bad Things,* and get the name and phone number of the builder, not the seller or developer, but the *builder*—and note the price.

While looking at an expensive house in a prestige neighborhood, we walked into the living room and a foot went through the floor. Obviously, it was only the incompleted subfloor that had given way at a weak place, we thought, and we made a note of it. Two months later on returning to the completed house, we admired the lovely living room carpet. But when we stood in the unfinished basement under the living room and looked up, there was the broken board, held in place by a single nail and merely covered with carpet! The subfloor was the *only* floor, and bright red carpet was visible through each wide crack! Carefully watching our step, we went through the house making notes. On leaving we had filled four pages under *Bad Things* and noted only one entry under *Good Things*—the house looked attractive from the street.

After inspecting a few houses you will become expert in knowing what to look for and where. This serious and essential task may become a game in which you can predict a certain item being one way or another. Your objective is to compare different builders by learning what kind of house they produce.

Take one builder and study his work. What kind of house does he build? Do you like what you see? Will it last and would you be proud to live in one like it? You should be concerned with two major aspects: (1) the building process and (2) the finished product. The latter may be your environment for the rest of your life, and it represents the largest financial investment of your lifetime. The former can be an exciting, happy experience, or it can wreck your physical and mental health beyond repair. You want to succeed in both.

LOOK FOR THESE

1. Have building debris and mud accumulated in the street and neighboring yards?

2. Have local ordinances concerning open burning and temporary electrical wires in public streets been violated?

3. Have new materials been dropped in mud, or have they been protected from weather?

4. Has the builder been sensitive to natural beauty and left some trees?

5.   Is the mortar of several different colors, obviously showing the work of different crews? Are masonry fireplaces lined with firebrick or common brick (which will crack and crumble)?

6.   Stand on the stoop and look up, down, and around. Does trim around the windows and door fit? Is there a gap at the bottom? Do wood and masonry joints fit snugly? Can birds and squirrels enter the attic through gaping holes at the eaves?

7.   Does the house shake when you shut the front door or when you walk across the floor?

8.   Does it have insulation? Everywhere? Or correct quality for your climate? Installed snugly from stud to stud?

9.   How tight is the subflooring? Is there one?

10.   Are there double joists at points of extra weight and strain —under walls, cabinetry, prefab fireplaces, and so on?

11.   Have split and broken studs been pieced together and used? Are window frames split or broken?

12.   Do studs and joists fit, or do they miss each junction by a half inch and are suspended by nails?

13.   Have load-bearing walls been cut into excessively by the plumber, electrician, and heating contractor?

14.   Are finished floors and ceramic tile protected from the workmen's muddy shoes?

15.   Have pennies been pinched in depth of closets, in width of hallways, stairs, and doors, and in size and quality of fixtures and appliances?

16.   Is there a deep musky smell in the basement and water or mud stains on basement walls and floors—indicating drainage problems?

17.   Did the builder put sheetrock under all paneling?

18.   Does the builder use paint and putty to cover a multitude of sins?

19.   Do windows and doors open and close easily, and do they lock?

20.   What is the quality of lighting fixtures, hardware, plumbing fixtures, carpeting, and so forth? Are they bottom-of-the-line?

21.   How do the workmen present impress you? Would you want *them* to build *your* house?

22.   Where does water from the roof drain? Into the basement, the neighbors' yards, the front door?

23.   Does the garage door close snugly and lock?

24.   What landscaping is provided?

25.   Does the builder proudly display his name in the front yard, or is he ashamed to claim the house?

After examining many houses by different builders, you will recognize recurring features. You will decide one builder is not for you, whereas another builds a good house and should be investigated further. Then begin the second stage of your detective work.

Contact the builder and give the first test. Tell him you are interested in his work, and request a list of his houses in different stages of construction, as well as finished ones, so you may examine them. If he hesitates, beware! But if he's anxious to show you all stages of his work and even gives names of people he has built for in the past, you can feel assured he is producing a product he is proud to present for close inspection.

Next, examine several of his houses in *all* stages of construction to see parts such as footing, framing, wiring, and plumbing that will be covered in the finished house. If possible, select a house he is building on speculation, and follow it step by step from beginning to completion. Observe:

1.   How long does it take him to complete the house? Do the men work regularly, or do they not show up for several weeks at a time? If a cloud passes over do they all lay off? And does work cease a week before and after every holiday?

2.   What quality of materials does he use in the areas that will be covered? Are they bottom-of-the-line or better?

3.   What type of workmanship does he accept? Do boards meet and corners fit? Are cracks caulked and cuts even? Does he demand and get good quality work? Do his workmen respect him?

4.   Does his work pass local inspections the *first time?*

5.   Are mistakes made frequently that have to be ripped out and done over?

6.   Does he plan the work in proper sequence to prevent one crew from tearing up the work of another to do their job? (One builder

we observed landscaped the same yard three times because he failed to have utility lines and the septic system installed first.)

7. Is there a great deal of scrap waste of materials indicating both poor estimates of quantities needed and careless inefficiency by the workmen? Do the workmen return after hours to help themselves to materials and appliances?

8. Does he make every effort to prevent accidents and theft at the site while at the same time carrying adequate insurance?

Following the construction of a specific house gives insight into the integrity of the builder that you would not otherwise gain. While inspecting a house we were "following," we found a kitchen window sill marred from having a board dragged in through it. The next week the entire sill had been replaced, although similar damages in other builders' houses were merely covered with paint.

Do the builder's houses work? Comments from people living in them can be used as an item of evaluation if the occupant is honest. Some will blame the builder for faults when their unrealistic demands created inevitable problems. Others will cover up serious mistakes and deceptions because they don't want it known that an unscrupulous builder made "fools of them." One Christmas, however, a large ad appeared in a newspaper, giving a feeling of confidence in one builder. It read:

> Thank you, _____ _____, for building us homes that will bring us endless joy throughout the years. Your concern and efforts on our behalf are appreciated.

It was signed by every person he had built for that year! This was an expression of extraordinary satisfaction because many relationships between builder and owner end in the courts.

Most established builders work in an area within reasonable driving distance from their home and office. Time and fuel are important commodities for the builder, and he must figure and plan his use of them carefully. If he spends too many hours driving to various building sites, he won't have adequate time to visit building supply companies, select materials properly, and supervise work on each house. Is your lot within his normal working range? If it's too far out of his way, he cannot visit it often, and during certain phases of construction the builder should inspect the house daily.

Some builders leave town rather than face consequences of their

Some builders confine themselves to their office and seldom visit the building site. Others take a personal interest in every house they build and inspect every aspect of the construction daily. This fireplace, ready for its stone facing, is being examined by the critical eye of the builder before further work continues.

work; others even leave the country! Such cases probably are rare, but you don't want to take the chance of becoming the victim of such a person, nor do you want to employ a builder who, you later discover, has a wide reputation for leaking roofs or other equally undesirable trademarks. What kind of reputation does the builder you are considering have? Does he complete houses he begins, or does he walk off the job if challenging problems develop? Does he consistently produce good quality work, and is he reliable? Call on your attorney and have him investigate to learn if the builder has been involved in litigation and why. Check local building associations and learn if the builder is a member in good standing, and ask for any other information they might give. If he's not a member, don't rush to negative conclusions. Some of the finest and most exclusive builders do not choose to affiliate with organizations, place their names in the yellow pages, or advertise elsewhere. Can you reach him readily by phone? The builder who has an unlisted telephone number and only a post office box address should be regarded with caution.

An excellent source of chatty information concerning a builder's reputation and general character is building supply company personnel. When looking at materials, engage the clerks in conversation, telling them who you are considering. Most will talk freely, and a composite of many conversations will indicate traits.

Does the builder take personal pride in each house he produces, or is each just another job? You want more than an assembly line attitude; you want personal attention to every detail by the expert. You will pay dearly for his services, and a well-built house costs no more (and often less) than a poorly built one.

Not every plan is buildable by every builder. Because of the reluctance of almost everyone to deviate from traditional style and design, many builders can construct only one basic style by one standard, basic method. Anything out of the ordinary causes a complete breakdown in communications before discussions have gotten underway. Is your house different from the thousands you see every day? How different is it, and what problems with construction and materials will be involved? You may think a nine-foot ceiling would create no problem, but it does because most paneling, sheetrock, studs, and other materials come in eight-foot lengths for constructing the standard eight-foot ceiling. You are limited by what your builder and his men *can* and *want* to do. Many builders don't want to bother with hunting out-of-the-ordinary materials or figuring out how to use them. They and their crews are "eight-foot men," and all walls they build are eight feet high. To build a nine-foot wall for you would be a nuisance, and why should they involve themselves with it when they can take another job with no "crazy" changes?

Some builders who cannot build anything but the standard house make every dwelling the same underneath. Only the outer surface and trim make one house appear different from the other. Such builders use the same materials and install the same fixtures in an inexpensive house as they do in one over $100,000—the latter just has more footage and fixtures. Some builders cannot read the details of architect's plans but have developed their own special methods of achieving the same end results. Does your proposed builder build by architect's plans? Or does he prefer designer's plans? And what would the price difference be between the two types? Ask him these questions:

1.   If he builds by architect's plans, will he follow every detail and method prescribed in the plans? Will this affect cost? Will he charge more if the architect supervises construction?

2.   Does he build by designer's plans?

3.   Does he have his own methods of construction, and does he take liberties to deviate from plans if his method will produce the same end result?

4.   Can he assure you that he can produce the house indicated by your plans?

5.   Will he warrant the house after it's built?

Go over your plans in detail with the builder, point out unique features, and observe his reactions. If he hesitates when confronted with out-of-the-ordinary features and tries to get you to change to the standard, he may not be the one for you. However, some builders welcome the change and challenge of something different, and even though they may never have built anything like it before, they jump in with enthusiasm.

Is your builder a carpenter who will work on the house along with his crews, or is he a businessman who leaves his comfortable office only occasionally to inspect the progress? Or is building just a lucrative side line, and does he give prime attention to his real profession? How many houses does he have going simultaneously? Can he *personally* supervise all of them? Ask him.

Who are your builder's workmen? Your house can be no better than the men who build it. The finest materials will produce no sounder house than the cheapest if they are poorly used. Many builders maintain a basic nucleus of workmen who are in their regular employ and move from house to house. These are dependable, reliable men the builder knows and trusts. They value their regular association with him, taking pride in producing a fine house and sharing in his good reputation. But who are the other men who will come and go, constructing 50 percent or more of your house? They are subcontractors, and it is they who might put the septic tank in uphill, hide electrical outlets behind paneling, fail to connect water pipes, uproot that thirty-foot dogwood tree while bringing

Does the builder display his name proudly at the building site? Or is he ashamed to claim the job?

in the gas line, or put the bathroom tile in the living room. A fine builder knows which subcontractors produce good work, are reliable, and fair. He will use them on a regular basis as he needs them, never employing unknown crews. Other builders pick up the cheapest crews from anywhere, accept any type work they do, pay half wages, and pocket the difference. This builder makes extra profit while you get an inferior house. Know in advance who will actually construct your house. Ask a builder about his men and observe them at work on someone else's house before selecting him.

Each builder is an individual. He has his likes and dislikes—he has a personality—and even though you have a contract stating that he will produce a house as specified, there are intangible areas that cannot be included in a written agreement. You must trust him in many matters and it is he, the person, who really produces a good or bad house, regardless of what the contract states. Study him, observe his work, and get to know him. Does he like your plans, and does he really want to build your house? Why? Would his crews actually be *able* to build it, and would they *want* to? Will he search for correct materials and give you the benefit of any money saved? Does he normally build in your price range, and how does his cost compare with estimates given by other builders? You don't necessarily want the lowest price, but you do want the best product for your money. If your builder is sensitive and feels as you do about your house—if there is rapport between you—then your wishes can be realized beyond your dreams.

19

HOW TO CUT COSTS

To get your first house bid, take your preliminary plans, along with specifications of individual items such as tile, appliances, paneling, light fixtures, and hardware, to your builder. He will study everything —conferring with suppliers and subcontractors—and return a bid that likely will be over budget. Inflation causes nearly every house to be over budget on the first bid. (Designers and architects recognize this and usually include one revision of plans at no extra charge.) If you and your planner have been closely attuned to the building market throughout the planning stage, your excess should not be great, and your problem of how to cut down should be a relatively minor one. However, if both of you have been drifting along in a make-believe world of financial fantasy, prepare for a shock. How stoically you can watch your dream disassembled and reconstructed in a less expensive form will be a test of your real convictions. You must do it, though, because *this is the point where most unbuilt dream homes fall apart.*

Waiting was once an alternative to cutting costs, but that is no longer possible. Building costs advance daily, making it impossible to wait a while, save a little more money, and then go ahead with your plans. Labor and material costs continue to go up as much as 1 percent per month (offsetting any possible drop in interest rates), and although you might accumulate several thousand dollars during a wait, the price of building will have increased even more. You may never live in your dream home if you don't cut down your plans to fit your *present* budget. Moreover, you will be comfortable in the knowledge that once your house payments start, rising building costs will no longer concern you. If you wait a year, your home could easily cost 12 percent more than presently and therefore be out of range forever.

Detach yourself from your emotional involvement, and analyze objectively the priority of your needs in relation to your plans. How would you cut costs on plans showing seven bathrooms, four guest rooms, and 5,500 square feet of floor space for a family of three? Obviously, you would slash off superfluous rooms and all that extra floor space. Yet the family who dreamed up that house is still living in an apartment while their plans gather dust in their architect's office. They just can't understand why the bids were over their limit of $70,000. Can you?

Don't feel embarrassed when you realize some features you've talked about to your friends are being dropped. It's your home, not theirs. You are building it and paying for it, and you need not explain or justify any of it to others.

Ponder several questions as you critically evaluate your plans, keeping in mind that labor and materials are both expensive commodities.

Have You Simply Overbuilt?

Take a little child through a toy shop and he will ask for everything he sees. His wonderment has no bounds—to him wishing makes it so. Adults are prone to be like children when planning a new home. In their wonderment they ask for everything they've seen, but wishing doesn't make it so in the adult world. Desires must be tempered to circumstances. Therefore, examine your plans for superfluous rooms. Don't sacrifice the whole house because of extra rooms that would be very nice but are not necessary.

Do You Really Need All That Footage?

Footage is the foundation of your cost. In all your excitement you may have added a foot here, another there, thinking that a foot of floor space requires just another foot of flooring material and nothing else. It isn't that simple. Each extra foot of floor space means more foundation, exterior walls, roofing, heating capacity, wiring, and plumbing. Adding footage increases your cost rapidly and similarly, cutting footage decreases cost instantly. If the per foot price in your area is $25, a mere 200 feet sliced off your plans will decrease the cost $5,000. Reducing a 40-foot by 35-foot floor plan to a 40-foot by 30-foot plan would be barely perceptible in the finished house. Yet the $5,000 cost reduction would be quite significant ($5 \times 40 \times \$25 = \$5,000$).

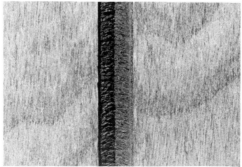

The price of interior paneling varies greatly—from $3.40 to $18.50 in the display at top. Look for a deep, disinct V-groove, as shown in the bottom photo; it can make inexpensive paneling look expensive.

This could amount to $40 a month difference in the mortgage payment that might be just the reduction you need. (A twenty-five-year loan at 8½ percent interest runs approximately $8 a month per $1,000 financed.)

Have You Demanded the "Best of Everything"?

"Monica has told our architect to put the best of everything in our house," our dinner guest related when we inquired as to the state of their project. A few months later he was muttering about the high cost of building delaying their house indefinitely. Monica apparently had not been willing to compromise on her best-of-everything demands.

Nearly all building supplies come in three different qualities—bottom-, middle-, and top-of-the-line. The price difference is staggering; you may find plywood paneling ranging from $2.98 to $125 per 4-foot by 8-foot sheet. A top-of-the-line, silent, colored water closet may be four times the price of the white, middle-of-the-line model, and yet both will perform the same utilitarian function. Likewise, prefab fireplaces range from under $100 to well over $1,000, and the sky is the limit on unique custom-built ones.

The key to having the appearance of the best of everything and not having to pay the price is to use the very best in selected, prominent spots. Carefully chosen middle- and bottom-of-the-line items used in company with the best will take on a reflected aura. For instance, if you must have the $125 rosewood paneling, use one piece over the fireplace, creating an extraordinarily beautiful focal point. Surrounding this with richly colored painted walls would be decidedly less expensive and equally as impressive as paneling the entire room at $125 a sheet.

Astute shoppers know that price does not always indicate quality. Brand name, design, origin, popularity, and what the market will bear are factors that influence the price tag on any item, whether it's a garment or building stone. A few days spent in comparison shopping for your finishing materials is a wise investment. You could easily turn up two kitchen light fixtures with identical electrical inner workings and both equally attractive to your eye that would differ in cost from $3.50 to $25.

Some areas of your home don't need the best of everything. Paneling or papering the insides of your closets is sheer luxury; if you are pushed financially, it is sheer folly. What about flooring? Do you plan to cover an expensive hardwood floor with wall-to-wall carpeting? If you've planned a lovely drapery and cornice window treatment that will cover the beautiful and expensive milled wooden window frames, why not economize and use an aluminum framed window instead?

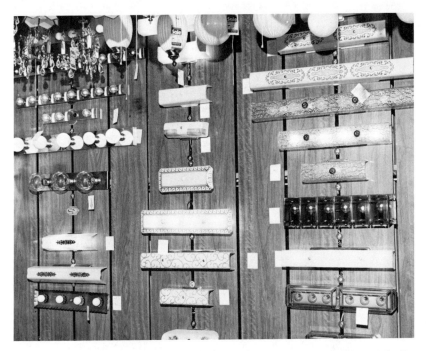

The prices of these bathroom fixtures range from $9 to $170 and bulbs are not included. Expect to spend $60 to equip your new house with bulbs.

The best of everything is wonderful if you can afford it. But if you can't, tone down your whole approach, keeping the best in choice spots and very carefully selecting substitute items from the middle- and bottom-of-the-line offerings for less conspicuous areas.

What Can You Easily Replace Later?

After you have lived in your home five years, you will have re-done all painted surfaces and refinished all floors. Your children's growth and ever-changing interests will probably necessitate continuous redecoration of their areas, and you yourself may desire a change here and there. All those items that you know will be replaced during the normal life of a house can be economy models initially, saving the greater expense until later when you may better afford it. If your mind is set on using $125 rosewood paneling for an entire room, paint now and plan to add the paneling in a few years when the paint becomes soiled and must be redone. Choose colorful, inexpensive, vinyl flooring for the present and add the $39.95-per-yard carpeting when the vinyl wears

A fireplace can be postponed and added later. It should be planned for in the basic house design to ensure adequate support and venting. A special spotlight focuses on the twelve foot chimney area which will feature a modern frieze. In the meantime, sculpture occupies the area.

out. Some items, such as windows, ceramic tile, and masonry, are generally never replaced, making their original installation permanent and their selection critical for appropriateness and durability for the life of the house.

Can You Postpone Something?

Postponing rooms or large individual items is one way of cutting costs without altering the total concept of the house. If you are adamant in not changing a thing in your plans, consider postponement as a method of bringing initial costs down. Rooms, even entire wings, can be delayed for several years to give you an opportunity to build now and start enjoying your home sooner. Swimming pools, greenhouses, fireplaces, cabinetry, bathrooms, appliances, air conditioning, electronic air cleaners, humidifiers, landscaping, and the finishing of basements, attics, or garages can be delayed easily. Include any postponed items in the original plans to ensure adequate supporting foundations, wiring, plumbing, heating capacity, and so on in the initial construction. Having to provide these items within the original house later could cause unnecessary difficulties.

Even though your planner and builder will gladly counsel you on how to cut down, ultimate decisions will be up to you. Carefully evaluate all methods and decide which ones can most successfully fit your house into your budget while causing the least disturbance to the total concept of your home.

20

INFLATION-FIGHTING SPECIFICS

You are acutely aware of what inflation is doing to your building costs. The following specific ideas will help you fight inflation now and continue working for you every time you make a mortgage payment.

THINGS THAT WILL SAVE MONEY

1. Pay loan closing costs only *once* by seeking a lender who makes combined construction-permanent loans. Paying closing costs on a construction loan, then on a permanent loan could cost several *thousand* dollars more.

2. Set up your own tax and insurance escrow savings account. Letting the lender hold it gives *him* 5½ percent interest that *you* could be drawing.

3. Avoid penalities by paying your mortgage on time.

4. Wise custom building is cheaper than buying a builder's speculation house because he must add his construction loan closing costs and interest, which could be $2,000 on a $45,000 house. Buying the same home through a realtor adds $2,250 more in a 5 percent realtor's fee.

5. Your financing will be cheaper if your home is similar to the standard for the area.

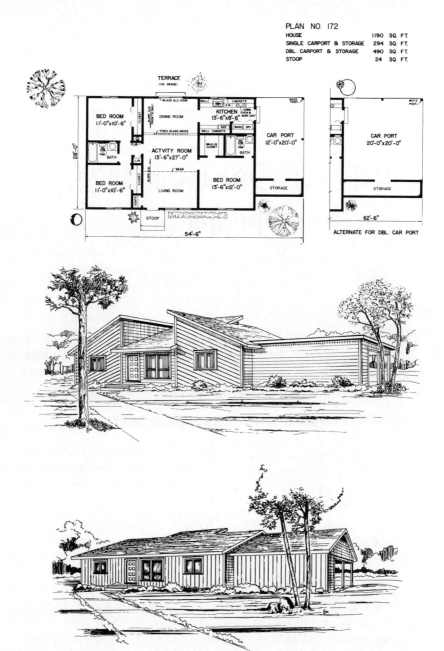

PLAN NO. 172

HOUSE	1190 SQ. FT.
SINGLE CARPORT & STORAGE	294 SQ. FT.
DBL. CARPORT & STORAGE	490 SQ. FT.
STOOP	24 SQ. FT.

TERRACE
(ON GRADE)

BED ROOM
11'-0"x10'-6"

DINING ROOM

KITCHEN
13'-6"x8'-6"

CAR PORT
12'-0"x20'-0"

ACTVITY ROOM
13'-6"x27'-0"

BATH

BATH

BED ROOM
11'-0"x10'-6"

LIVING ROOM

BED ROOM
13'-6"x12'-0"

STORAGE

STOOP

28'-0"

54'-6"

CAR PORT
20'-0"x20'-0"

STORAGE

62'-6"

ALTERNATE FOR DBL. CAR PORT

Save money by eliminating excess hall, foyer, and room-dividing walls as shown in this plan. Division of the activity room into a living room and dining room is created by a sloped ceiling and clerestory windows. Furniture placement can emphasize the division further, without adding to building costs. (Courtesy of W. D. Farmer, Residence Designer, Inc.)

6. Building in a recession is a buyer's market. Lenders lower interest rates to attract customers. Builders and laborers, glad to find work, also cut their profits.

7. Interior walls cost money. Eliminate needless halls and foyers and combine rooms, using furniture placement or room dividers to separate areas.

8. Interior doors cost at least $60 a unit and restrict air circulation. Don't use them if they aren't needed.

9. Don't pay for materials you don't use. If you make a room 12 feet wide, it takes a 14-foot floor joist, with 1½ feet cut off. Reducing that room's inside dimension to 11′ 6″ means you can use a 12-foot floor joist with no waste. Your planner should use this principle throughout the house. All plans illustrated in this book are based on this principle of economic use of materials.

10. Use ready-made plans. They cost less than $75.

11. Or have custom plans drawn by a residence designer.

12. Using the cube principle in design cuts building costs and heat loss.

13. Contemporary is cheaper to build and furnish than traditional styles.

14. Use art and signature items you already have instead of purchasing new ones.

15. Below-grade living space is cheaper than on-grade or above-grade space because it doesn't need exterior finishing materials.

16. A spiral stair saves space and money, but don't use it for the only access to an area.

17. Build only what *you* need, not what past generations needed.

18. Planning baths, kitchen, and laundry so that plumbing can be back-to-back in a common wall saves material and labor.

19. Substitute cheaper materials for more expensive ones, especially in large areas. For example, select a design where roofing comes down the outside wall; it's cheaper than any other exterior wall surface.

20. When you reduce room sizes to save money, using light colors on floors, walls, and ceilings makes rooms seem larger.

21. Omit the guest room. Use cots, sleeping bags, or a motel.

22.   Shade trees save air conditioning money.

23.   Anything that saves labor saves money.

24.   Stock items are cheaper than specially ordered or custom-made ones (cabinetry is an exception).

25.   Prefab fireplaces are cheaper than masonry ones, and they are guaranteed to work!

26.   Individual smoke detectors (about $30) strategically placed are cheaper than a smoke detection system, even when the smoke detection system is installed as part of a security system.

27.   Not only are recessed lights cheaper than most light fixtures, but they save space and money used for tables and lamps.

28.   Dimmers cost a few dollars more than ordinary light switches, but they save electricity.

29.   Double glazing with removable panes is cheaper than sealed insulating glass, but it works just as well.

30.   Concrete blocks are the cheapest building material.

31.   Plastic plumbing pipes cost less to buy, use, and transport than heavier cast iron. Plastic also lasts longer and doesn't clog up as often.

32.   Good shopping habits pay off when buying building materials. You and your builder should look for sales, samples, close-outs, discontinued models, and volume discounts.

33.   Prices on building materials vary greatly, but the following relationships are usually true: Imported ceramic tile is cheaper than domestic tile; chrome bath fittings are cheaper than any other finish; pine and fir cost less than cedar or redwood; wood is cheaper than masonry; wallpaper costs less than fabric wall coverings and paint is cheaper than either; and vinyl asphalt tile is the least expensive of all floor coverings.

34.   Investigate synthetic materials. Not only are most of them cheaper, but they're usually more durable too. Molded plastic tub and shower units cost less than cast iron units surrounded with tile. You can save money by using interior door units covered with masonite. Philippine mahogany plywood layers covered with a printed vinyl becomes plywood "paneling" at $3 to $4 a sheet. It matches, stacks, and cleans better than middle-of-the-line real plywood paneling at $12 to $15 a sheet.

35.   Processed materials are usually cheaper and also acquire desirable characteristics during the processing. Exterior fir paneling is

Double glazing with removable panes is about 20 percent cheaper than the sealed variety. The pane locks in place and can be removed easily for cleaning.

cheaper to buy, handle, and install than any kind of wood siding. It is also fire, mildew, moisture, and insect resistant. No wood has these properties naturally.

36. You will save money now and on future repairs by hiring a competent builder.

37. Concrete slab floors are less expensive than joist wooden floors.

38. Simplicity is synonymous with savings. Simple trim moldings will not cost as much to buy or install as elaborate trims bought as stock items or custom made in specialty woodworking shops.

39. Ignore "cost-cutting" advice from your friends, relatives, and neighbors. Pay heed only to your lender, planner, and builder.

40.   Relocate north windows on the south to obtain a net heat gain instead of loss from your glass.

41.   Buying land that requires little alteration will save on grading and landscaping expenses.

42.   Basic landscaping, grading, and walls will cost far less at building time when men and equipment are already at the site.

43.   Natural landscaping is cheap and requires little attention. You must, however, buy a lot with nice trees and small plants already there.

44.   Don't incorporate natural boulders, streams, or trees into your home. Such features look pretty in the magazines, but they are an endless source of problems and an extraordinary expense.

45.   Plan your windows and place your home on your lot so that privacy screens are unnecessary.

46.   Your fire insurance will be less if you are within 1,000 feet of a fire hydrant and within three miles of a fire station.

47.   The more fire resistant your roof is, the less your fire insurance premium will be.

48.   If you take a larger deductible than the standard policy offers, your homeowner's insurance will be cheaper.

THINGS THAT MIGHT SAVE MONEY

1.   The first lots in a new subdivision might be cheaper to encourage sales.

2.   The last lots might be reduced to get rid of them. Be careful!

3.   "Cheap" country land may not be cheap when you figure costs of daily transportation, building a road in, bringing in utilities, and getting workmen and materials from the city.

4.   A lot in a subdivision is usually the best buy, but if development is not complete and you have to pay extra fees to bring in utilities, think again.

5.   Security, fire, and sanitary services are usually cheaper if they are provided through taxes rather than by private firms.

6.   Low tax areas are no bargain if they provide no services, and they are only a temporary bargain if everyone else is moving in there too. It's just a matter of time until all of you will be paying for

the schools, roads, sewers, and traffic lights that your presence there demands.

7.   If your tax appraisal is based on the number of rooms in your home, great rooms and other combined rooms can realize substantial savings. Open planning in one $150,000 home created only *four* rooms. To the tax office it was the same as a cottage.

8.   Go to the tax office and inspect your tax appraisal carefully for measurements, materials, and items. If the appraiser filled in your form at the neighborhood coffee shop instead of visiting your premises, you may be taxed indefinitely for items *not* in your home.

9.   Appeal all reassessments you ever get. Many tax offices automatically grant a reduction to anyone who appeals—just to keep them quiet.

10.   Even though easy-care surfaces may cost more, they will save money if they eliminate hiring domestic help.

11.   Industrial materials may cost less than comparable residential ones. But be careful. If they don't fit into the standard two-by-four construction you will have problems.

12.   Living close to the point of manufacture usually brings down the retail price of carpet, appliances, and building materials. You may also visit the factory sales room for cheap usable seconds and rejects.

13.   Prefab construction is very popular for vacation homes. It may save money on your family home if you live close enough to the factory so that transportation expenses are not excessive. Get exact costs on everything you have to provide such as clearing, grading, foundation, utilities, electricity, heating, and plumbing. Also determine if there is enough flexibility of plans to suit your needs.

14.   Solar heating may save money.

15.   A basement costs more, but it can be a saving if it substitutes for areas you would have put above grade.

16.   Decks also are an expense if they are superfluous, but decking and glass can psychologically extend a living area, allowing you to reduce its real size.

17.   Building during the winter might save money because it's the off-season. But the builder has to provide temporary heat, erosion control, and additives to keep mortar from freezing. Labor, however, should be cheaper, unless the men have gone south to work in the citrus groves.

THINGS THAT WON'T SAVE MONEY

1. Hiring an architect won't save money; it will cost thousands!

2. Serving as your own contractor will not save money. Subcontractors will know you are inexperienced and price their work accordingly. Supply houses will extend you no special prices, and they may even unload shoddy materials on you.

3. Trying to be one of your craftsmen is equally as foolish unless you have proven experience in the craft. Lenders do not gamble on unproven craftsmen.

4. Don't try to draw your own plans or hire a friend who has had a course or two in drafting or architecture. Good plans involve far more than a pleasing placement of rooms. They must conform to standard lumber sizes and building methods to be workable. Only an experienced designer can achieve this.

5. Oddball materials make nice copy for the press, but trying to insulate with rolled-up newspaper or using empty bottles and oil drums for walls in your home will never get past the building inspectors or lenders. (Instead, try oddball ideas on a lien-free vacation house out of range of building codes.)

6. Make your home meet your needs and reflect your tastes, but avoid nonconventional "kooky" custom-made items. They add to your costs.

7. Special ordering costs more.

8. Inexpensive materials are not cheap if their installation runs the total cost above the usual. For example, old brick may be inexpensive, but the hand labor necessary to clean off old mortar makes them cost more installed than new ones.

9. When constant professional maintenance is required by a cheap material, it's not a bargain.

10. "Helping" the workmen follow the plans won't save money or anything else.

STOP! REEVALUATE

Stop! Don't sign any papers yet. Reevaluate the entire project. Find a quiet place somewhere, sit down, and carefully review once again the papers, plans, and samples you have collected. Thus far you have not signed a building contract, nor have you made formal application for your loan. Design fees are the only monies you have obligated, and should you decide to drop the project now, your financial loss will be small. Later, it will be a different story.

Ask yourselves once more, "Is this really the home we want?" Your ideas have gone through many stages of evolution since you first said, "Let's build a new house!" Has that evolution been in the right direction, adapting your thoughts to your environment, yielding a pleasing plan; or has it somewhere turned down a blind alley leading away from your desires?

Your original idea was to build a home to meet your family's needs. Review the needs that you carefully identified in the initial planning stages, and ask the following questions:

1. Are the family's needs met in the present plan?

2. Have our needs changed since we started?

3. Will we be able to live our desired new life style in this house?

4. Has anyone high-pressured us into decisions we dislike?

5. Have we retained the original concept and feeling throughout changes and compromises?

6. Is our signature on the house?

7. Will it work for us better than a ready-built house?

8. Will it use energy efficiently?

9. Can our family be safe, secure, and healthy in this house?

10. Will we be proud of it? Will it give us the identity we desire?

11. Have we been innovative in solving problems?

12. Did we survey all materials available before choosing our favorites?

13. Will housekeeping and maintenance be easy?

14. Does our lighting enhance the beauty and utility of our home? Is it economical financially and energy-wise?

15. Do landscaping, lot, and house form a compatible and pleasing unit?

16. Can we really afford it? Have we remembered to estimate

utilities, garden supplies, gasoline, insurance, taxes, furniture, draperies, linens, door mats, garbage cans, and mail box?

17. Have we the time and enthusiasm to go on?

18. Do we trust our builder?

19. Have we made the best possible financial arrangement?

20. Does our home really thrill us?

21. Are we sure we want to go through with it?

Remember, *there's no point in building if you can't have what you want*. So now when your plans are complete, your builder chosen, and a firm bid in hand, but *no contract signed,* pause long enough to reevaluate the whole project. It is your life that will be lived in this home, and your toil that will pay for it. Is it what *you* want?

21

BUILDING
CONTRACT

Whereas no business agreement should be entered into without legal counsel, you must ask your attorney to draw up a building contract for your home. His professional obligation is to protect *you and your interests,* and his fee is a small price to pay for that protection. Although mutual trust must always exist between owner and builder, or they cannot hope to work together successfully, a professionally drawn contract does not in any way imply a lack of this trust. Rather, it is a written statement signed, sealed, and witnessed, attesting to this mutual trust in the undertaking of a major business agreement.

Your building contract will be drawn up in accord with the laws of your area, and it should include these basic items:

1. Names of the owner and builder, and date.

2. Identification of the land.

3. Statement that the builder will build the house in accord with the plans and specifications.

4. Inclusion of the plans and specifications as a part of the contract.

5. Procedure for changes.

6. Time limit on construction.

7. Price and manner of payment.

8. Responsibility for various fees and insurance.

9.   Statement that all bills are to be paid.

10.   Signatures of owner and builder.

The following contract is an example of one containing all essentials:

STATE OF GEORGIA
COUNTY OF ANYWHERE

(1   Names of the owner and builder, and date)

THIS AGREEMENT made and entered into this the —— day of December, 1977, by and between U.S. CITIZEN, Party of the First Part, hereinafter referred to as "Owner," and JOHN DOE, Party of the Second Part, hereinafter referred to as "Contractor."

(2   Identification of the land)

WITNESSETH: That,

WHEREAS, Owner has fee simple title to a tract of land in Land Lot 217 of the 18th District of Anywhere County, Georgia, and being Lot 26 Block LL, Good Estates, Unit XVII, according to a deed recorded at Deed Book 2479, Page 270, Anywhere County Records, upon which he desires a house to be erected, and

WHEREAS, Contractor has agreed to erect a house on said lot for the consideration shown hereinbelow;

NOW, THEREFORE, in consideration of the premises and in further consideration of the mutual benefits flowing to each of the Parties hereto,

IT IS AGREED AS FOLLOWS:

(3   Statement that the builder will build the house in accord with the plans and specifications)

1.   Contractor agrees to provide all labor and material and to do all things necessary to properly erect on said lot a house built in accordance with: (a) The plans on file with ————— SAVINGS AND

LOAN ASSOCIATION, the same being Plan No. 2331 prepared by R. S. Designer; and

(4 Inclusion of the plans and specifications as a part of the contract)

(b) The specifications on file with ———— SAVINGS AND LOAN ASSOCIATION. Said plans and specifications are incorporated herein by reference and made a part of this agreement to the same extent as if they were set forth in full herein.

(5 Procedure for changes)

2. No changes which have not already been made in the terms herein, plans, and specifications shall be made in the future unless the same shall be agreed to in writing by both Parties.

3. Contractor convenants that he will furnish his best skill and judgment in the performance of this agreement and in the construction of said house.

(6 Time limit on construction)

4. Construction of the house shall begin as of date of execution and Contractor covenants that the same shall be completed on or before 150 days from date of execution, weather permitting.

(7 Price and manner of payment)

5. Owner shall pay Contractor for his services $—— in the following manner:
(a) Owner has this date deposited with Contractor $—— as earnest money, the sum shall be credited toward the final payment of the above mentioned contract price.
(b) Owner will attempt to secure from ———— SAVINGS AND LOAN ASSOCIATION a combination Construction–Permanent Loan in the principal amount of $—— of which the sum of $——- will be available in the Due Borrower's Account for disbursement in accordance with the Disbursement Schedule of the Association as construction progresses. If said loan is secured, Owner will authorize the Association to make disbursements to the Contractor from this Construction Loan Account, and the amount actually disbursed by the Association to the Contractor shall be a credit against the total contract price. If said loan is not secured, this contract becomes null and void.

(c) Upon completion of construction and upon final approval by the Association and by the Inspection Department of Anywhere County, this contract will be considered to be substantially completed whereupon Owner will pay Contractor the difference between the earnest money mentioned in Item (a) above, the amount received by the Contractor from the Association in accordance with Item (b) above, and the contract price.

(8   Responsibility for various fees and insurance)

(d) All loan costs, interest costs, and survey costs shall be the obligation of Owner.

(e) Builder agrees to indemnify and hold owner blameless from any acts or claims arising out of or in the course of construction of said dwelling. Builder further agrees to insure said dwelling during the course of its construction against fire and other hazards.

(9   Statement that all bills are to be paid)

(f) At the time of final payment Contractor shall give Owner a properly sworn affidavit that all bills incurred for labor and materials have been paid in full.

IN WITNESS WHEREOF, the Parties have hereunto set their hands and affixed their seals on the day and year first above set out.

(10   Signatures of owner and builder)

_____ (SEAL)

U. S. CITIZEN, Owner

_____ (SEAL)

JOHN DOE, Contractor

After you have made your second trip to the lender and you, your lender, builder, planner, and attorney are satisfied with your house and its price, you are ready to sign the building contract.

PART 3

BUILDING PROCESS

22

STEP-BY-STEP BUILDING

Are *batter boards* gourmet cooking utensils? No, they are boards used in defining the perimeter of your house. Likewise, *footings* have nothing to do with shoes and socks but are a part of the foundation resting in the ground. And don't expect a *joist* to be a tilt between dueling knights; it's a piece of lumber used in framing. A brief glimpse at the sequential steps in building a house will give you an idea of what to expect when construction begins. Work falls into three major divisions:

- Getting the house out of the ground

- Roughing it in

- Finishing it out

Your house may require a slightly different order or additional steps, or you may need to use a new technique to construct some unique feature. Most building proceeds along the following steps:

GETTING THE HOUSE OUT OF THE GROUND

Weather determines the speed of progress at this stage when men and machines have no protection from the elements. Work may stop for days at a time while your builder waits for the ground to dry from heavy rains, or you may be blessed with weather good enough to speed through this stage in two or three weeks.

Staking It Out

When you've decided on the placement of the house, it's time to mark the corners with wooden stakes for the clearing and grading crews. Do this yourself, or be with your builder when he does it, because the misplacement of the house is one mistake that cannot be corrected after construction has begun. Block your house outline into workable rectangles if projections and wings give it an unwieldy shape, and proceed to measure off the outside dimensions, driving wooden stakes at the corners. Check your accuracy by measuring the two diagonals of your rectangles. If your measurements are accurate and your corners right angles, the two diagonals will be equal. If not, the longer diagonal will be in the direction of the list. Move the stakes until the diagonals become equal.

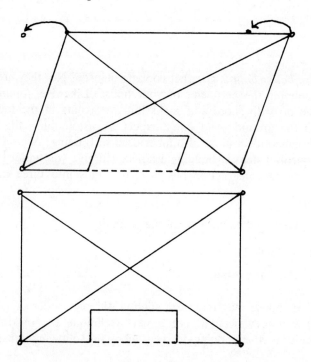

Allow a minimum of 3 feet between the house and trees you want to save to enable workmen to move about freely.

Clearing and grading machinery must have a path to the building site, so stake out your drive to be cleared and graded at the same time as the house and used as the pathway for machinery.

Clearing

Agree with the builder on one system of marking trees—mark either those to be saved or those to be removed. Then stay around while the clearing crew works. Ask them to remove dead or diseased trees that might endanger the house during summer hurricanes or winter storms. The men will be glad to do this. Later, after the house is built, removing trees could be a difficult and costly undertaking.

Grading

Leveling the site for your house takes a day or two. A bulldozer moves the earth as needed for the foundation (cutting down or building up), following closely the stakes you placed.

Batter Boards

The batter board crew (they are very specialized in the building industry) will erect wooden corners about a foot outside the perimeter of the house. The crew will precisely measure and attach strings from corner to corner, accurately locating the perimeter walls, defining the corners, and leveling the floor.

Footing

A narrow trench under the batter board string will be dug by the footing crew. The floor of the trench is always level; thus when the footing goes down a slope, it does so in steps. Once the footing trenches are correctly dug, concrete of the necessary strength for your soil and house will be poured into them, making a base around the entire perimeter and under each supporting pier. Composition of the footing as well as its size usually is controlled by local building codes, and official inspection and approval may be necessary before work can proceed beyond this point.

Foundation Walls and Piers

Slowly the house begins to rise out of the ground as foundation walls and piers are built. Cement blocks, brick, stone, and poured concrete are the usual materials with waterproofing going on the outside of all below-grade living space walls.

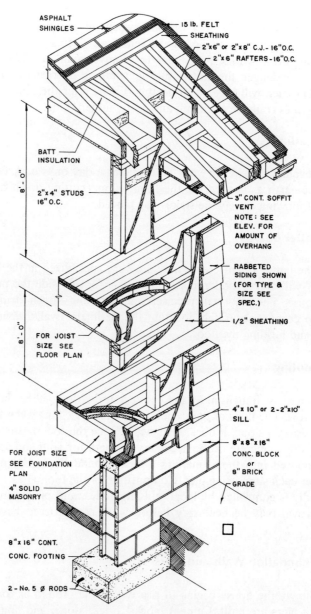

ASPHALT
SHINGLES

15 lb. FELT

SHEATHING

2"x6" or 2"x8" C.J.-16"O.C.

2"x6" RAFTERS-16"O.C.

BATT
INSULATION

8'-0"

2"x4" STUDS
16" O.C.

3" CONT. SOFFIT
VENT

NOTE: SEE
ELEV. FOR
AMOUNT OF
OVERHANG

RABBETED
SIDING SHOWN
(FOR TYPE &
SIZE SEE
SPEC.)

1/2" SHEATHING

8'-0"

FOR JOIST
SIZE SEE
FLOOR PLAN

4"x 10" or 2-2"x10"
SILL

8"x 8"x 16"

CONC. BLOCK
or
8" BRICK

FOR JOIST SIZE
SEE FOUNDATION
PLAN

GRADE

4" SOLID
MASONRY

8"x16" CONT.
CONC. FOOTING

2 - No. 5 ⌀ RODS

Exterior walls cover the many other materials used in constructing your home, as shown by this cutaway drawing. (Courtesy of W. D. Farmer, Residence Designer, Inc.)

Slab Floors

Concrete slab floors may have plumbing pipes, radiant heat coils, or even electric conduits buried inside, and these must be laid before the floor is poured. After pouring, the concrete will be smoothed and allowed to cure for about a day. Don't fret if it rains immediately after the pouring, because this won't inhibit the chemical reaction taking place in the concrete.

ROUGHING IT IN

Until now, your building site has resembled a surrealist landscape more than your dream home, but once the framing crew arrives the pace will quicken and the metamorphosis will begin.

Framing

The framing crew is the most important crew. They give shape and substance to your home by erecting subfloors, walls, and roof. Much of the subsequent work is dependent on the accuracy and quality of the framing. Almost like magic the walls go up as a pile of lumber becomes the skeleton of your home. Quick! If you want to move a window or door, do it now before the studs and headers are all in place. There will be a frantic race to get the house "under roof," then a sigh of relief as weather will no longer be of such great importance.

Drying It In

As soon as the framing is up, the exterior walls and roof will be covered with the water repellent materials that underlie the finished exterior surfaces (brick, paneling, shingles, etc.), making the house dry enough for interior work and storage of materials. Window units and interior doors, usually shipped as ready-to-use units, can be hung now.

Plumbing, Heating, and Electricity

No sooner does the framing crew get the wall sections secured than their handiwork is seemingly destroyed by a horde of workmen with drills and saws who descend like a swarm of termites. Plumbers, electricians, and heating men must cut through walls and floors to install all pipes and wires before the walls are closed up. Telephone wires, central vacuum, and burglar alarm systems will go in now.

Wiring follows framing. Holes are drilled through studs and joists to provide raceways for electrical and telephone wires.

Insulation

After all necessary pipes and wires have gone into exterior walls and roof sections, insulation can be put up. It should fit snugly from stud to stud with every chink and cranny filled.

Exterior Walls

At any time after drying in, exterior walls can be finished. Masonry fireplaces will be built now, and prefab fireplaces can go in now or later, depending upon their design. Exterior wood surfaces should be painted as soon as possible to seal them from the weather.

FINISHING IT OUT

Finishing crews are craftsmen, working with a refinement not necessary in previous work. They will be slow and meticulous, as piece by piece your home develops. The scheduling of their work will differ according to the materials you have chosen, usually leaving the most fragile until the last to prevent its soiling.

Walls and Ceilings

Sheetrock will be nailed over studs, and tape and "mud" will be used to cover the seams so skillfully that they cannot be detected in finished walls. If your plans call for wet plaster instead of dry wall (sheetrock) construction, that will be done now by applying wet plaster over wire mesh nailed to the studs.

Cabinetry

Kitchen and bathroom cabinetry usually is made to measure in a cabinet shop and brought to the building site ready to install. It should be in place before adjacent ceramic tile or paneling is installed.

Ceramic Tile

You will be getting anxious to see something completed, and the ceramic tile will come at just the right time. It is laid early in the finishing process, and its color and sheen will foretell more lovely things to come.

Plumbing Fixtures

Plumbers will return, laden this time with crates and boxes, to install plumbing fixtures. It's also their job to install hot water heaters and dishwashers, although other crews must connect these appliances to power sources. Your baths and kitchen begin to take on a finished look with tile, cabinets, and fixtures in place.

Wall Surfaces

What did you choose for your wall surfaces—paneling, paper, fabric, or paint? Specialized crews will begin covering your walls and others will add refined trim molds around ceilings, doors, and windows. (It's time now to be fussy about fingerprints.)

Appliances and Mechanical Equipment

Built-in appliances, furnaces, and air conditioners can be installed at any time after their bases are prepared, but many builders will wait until there are locks on the outside doors.

Flooring

Do you have wooden, poured plastic, or terrazzo floors? They will go in early because the sanding and finishing are messy. Vinyl and carpeting are relatively clean and simple to install and might not go down until just before moving day. Ask your builder to put paper over all finished floors to protect them from muddy feet.

Hardware

Some builders put temporary locks on all outside doors as soon as they are hung. However, permanent locks and door knobs usually are added after the doors are painted. Bathroom hardware, towel bars, paper holders, and soap dishes can be installed at any time after the walls are finished.

Light Fixtures

Grotesque wires have projected from each electrical receptacle since the electricians' first visit during the framing, defying your imagination to visualize beautiful fixtures in their places. At last, when almost everything else is done, the electrician will return to hang your fixtures, and with that your house will come alive!

Utility Lines

Water, gas, sewer, and septic lines can be laid at almost any stage of building. Be present for all this if you want to protect trees or natural areas, especially when crews are sent by utility companies rather than subcontracted by your builder. Utility company workers are far removed from your dream home and will likely have little feeling for your landscaping, purchased or natural.

Drive

You may have wondered, as you slipped and slid down your muddy drive, when you would get a permanent one. Your builder is just as anxious as you, and he will build it as soon as possible after the heavy trucks have stopped making deliveries. When the drive, walks, stoops, and steps are built, tracked-in mud will decrease sharply.

Landscaping

After the last digging machine has left, the landscaping crew can begin. They will start by back-filling the house, carefully pushing dirt against the foundation. Many builders wrap the lower portion of the house in plastic to keep it clean at this point. Small tractors will be used to smooth over the disturbed earth, hauling in more earth when needed. Planting and design will follow your carefully conceived plan. Don't forget to water the new plantings! It's easy to overlook this essential duty if the landscaping is done a few weeks before moving.

Cleanup

Is the house ready for you? Not quite. The last crew to work will be the cleanup crew, scrubbing and polishing everything just for you. They will remove the last muddy footprint, wash the windows, and clean the baths. When they finish, your home will be ready for you to move into.

23

RELATIONSHIPS WITH WORKMEN

Whatever you do, don't plant yourself at the building site daily with plans in hand, following nail by nail each workman's job, as one detail-conscious fashion designer did. Then every evening her perfectionist husband came out with a sledge hammer and knocked loose all the "mistakes." They both were completely bewildered when workmen walked off the job calling it quits. News travels fast among construction crews. No one else would touch the job, and the couple was faced with the arduous task of doing it themselves, or never being able to move in. Now, seven years later, they are still driving out from their apartment and pegging away on weekends and holidays with no end in sight. Their children have grown up and left for college, having never lived in the home so carefully planned for their childhood years.

This overanxious couple failed to realize one simple fact, and their builder neglected to tell them: There are several good ways to approach any step in building, and daily, unpredictable variations of weather, supplies, and crews may make a change of procedure from the plans necessary. This often results in a better house for the owner, such as a concrete basement floor poured over steel forms instead of the specified fill dirt when endless rains made hauling dirt impossible. The builder lost money on that change, but it was the only way to proceed with the house during unusually wet weather.

Equally as foolish as the overanxious couple was the young psychiatrist who thought he had a sure-fire method of avoiding all home-building traumas by not visiting the building site at all until everything was completed. On moving day he toured his home for the first time with obvious pleasure until he stepped into the downstairs family room, and there, not in the adjoining half-bath, stood the water closet firmly embedded in the concrete floor! There was nothing to do but plant a water lily in it and hope no one pulled the handle.

There are times to be a perfectionist, but when you are building your home you must remember that workmen are human, materials are not precision made, and earth and sky are totally unpredictable. Therefore, perfection is impossible, but excellence is obtainable, and this is what you deserve and should strive for. Your relationships with workmen will greatly influence the completion and quality of your home.

Good workmen are a proud lot. They are craftsmen, frequently having spent a lifetime in their specialty. Sorry workmen are abominable. They are often shiftless scoundrels, drifting from town to town to avoid the clutches of the law. The latter group gets notoriety and causes a cloud of scorn to be cast over all. The only way to avoid sorry workmen on the job is to employ a reputable builder whom you can trust in turn to hire reputable workmen.

When we say reputable, we're referring only to the quality of their work and their trustworthiness on the job—not education, intelligence, personal habits, or even morals, because these things have little to do with their building ability. The finest framing crew we've known had surprising personal habits and were almost totally illiterate, reading well enough only to interpret plans. But they could solve structural problems with a ruler and saw that stumped many professionals. They were much in demand, and one was truly lucky to have them frame his home.

Any parent knows bribery may get temporary results with a child, but each time the demand is a little larger and the child's respect for the parent a little less. Bribes on the job work the same way, so beware of plying the workmen with beer and liquor, thinking you are buying a better job. One architect, acting as his own contractor to save money, tried this approach and soon found his liquor bill larger than his labor bill and the house listing to one side. The men had reached the point where they *wouldn't* work if he didn't treat them and *couldn't* work if he did! Genuine respect and sincere compliments are the only things to give workmen, and these should be given freely. Good workmen will rise to a challenge and do an even better job if they know you really appreciate their efforts.

Visit the building site daily if at all possible to let them know you care, but don't stay so long that they feel you are trying to supervise. Know your plans so well you don't have to bring them along to check details, and if measurements look askew, wait until after quitting time to bring out your tape measure. Neither white collar professional men nor ladies are supposed to know anything at all about construction, and

Inspect the work on your house daily—after workmen have gone. Check dimensions, workmanship, materials, and every item of equipment. If something is amiss, make a note of it and tell the builder when both you and he are relaxed. Don't point out errors to workmen.

therefore they should never openly question or criticize a workman's job if they want the work to continue. These comments should be saved for the builder who will tactfully give them to his men. Varying the time of your visit can pay dividends and may prevent an unscrupulous workman from concealing (rather than correcting) a mistake by anticipating your visit at a certain hour. One owner dropped by his site during his lunch hour and found workmen hastily slapping plaster over a huge crack in a supporting wall made by a runaway bulldozer. Had he waited until his usual visiting hour that day he would never have known that concealed within the wall lay damage with a potential for infinite trouble later.

Your key to successful relationships is: OBSERVE, DON'T SUPERVISE. Talk with the builder often and let him explain anything you don't understand, but in talking with him, don't give him bad news until after he's eaten his dinner. If you have something really disturbing to discuss, be sure you've had your dinner too, and give your builder a chance to relax with a few cocktails, tranquilizers, and dull TV shows. Avoid any major confrontations during rainy weather, because that brings much of his work to a sliding halt, and even the most personable fellow becomes a grump then.

Pessimists say a compromise is a deal in which no one wins. Optimists say it's a deal in which no one loses, and this is a definition to keep in mind constantly as your home progresses. Unanticipated events will occur in which you will have to choose between forcing the builder to the letter of the contract or making a compromise. If the total effectiveness of the house will not be hurt by a compromise, be ready and willing to make one. A unique custom glass door was made and installed backward in one contemporary house. To have reordered the door would have cost the builder several hundred dollars and several months delay. Weighing these facts against using the backward door, the owner found neither the aesthetics, the structure, nor the effectiveness of the dwelling was harmed, so he compromised and accepted the door. No one lost.

Once building is underway you and your family will want to do everything possible to keep things moving along. Keep children out of the way, and don't borrow tools and supplies from the workmen. Because this project is a business deal, and a very big and important one for you, avoid getting on a first-name basis with anyone. The potency of any reprimand you have to make is diminished by the casualness of first names.

24

FINAL INSPECTION

During the course of construction, your house will have many inspections by people interested in the project. Your lender will inspect for progress and justified cost of work before disbursing funds. Local authorities will be concerned with compliance with local building codes, and the VA and FHA will look for compliance with their regulations, if you have a VA or FHA loan. You and the builder will inspect regularly from the beginning, and with so many inspections, most errors will be caught and remedied quickly. Nevertheless, one last and final inspection should be made by you, the owner, to satisfy yourself that your home is complete in every detail and ready to start serving you in the manner you have planned.

This inspection will be concerned primarily with how your house looks and operates because most of the vital structural and functional components will have been inspected earlier and sealed within walls, ceilings, and floors. Use the following checklist in your final inspection as you carefully and slowly inspect for the last time:

1. Have all terms of your contract been met? Has any item in your specifications been omitted?

2. Have all utilities—water, gas, electricity, telephone—been turned on and listed in your name? Have construction bills been paid?

3. How does the workmanship look? Are all gaps in the wood trim filled and finished? Does the floor tremble when you jump in the

center? How about seams in finishing materials—do they stick out like sore thumbs, or are they neatly concealed? How many coats of paint did you finally get? Everywhere? Did the painter remember to plug all nail holes and cover them? Does the vinyl flooring lie flat? Is there padding under the carpet, and is it all tight?

4.   Is the weatherstripping tight around all doors?

5.   Was the insulation installed in the ceiling?

6.   Are heat and air conditioning ducts insulated?

7.   Do you have all necessary attachments in bathrooms and vanities?

8.   Where are the window screens?

9.   Has the cleanup crew cleaned all windows inside and outside (even the high ones) and bathrooms?

10.   Have workmen removed all their equipment and supplies, leaving only those remnants of paint and paper that you requested?

11.   Has protective paper been placed on floors to prevent movers from soiling them?

12.   Do you have all keys and do they work smoothly in the locks?

13.   Ring your door bells. Can you hear them?

14.   Can you open and close all windows, doors, cabinets, and drawers smoothly?

15.   Do you know how to operate the dishwasher, stove, disposer, central vacuum, furnace, and air conditioner? Run all appliances and mechanical equipment through a normal working cycle. Do they work?

16.   Are all toilets, tubs, basins, and sinks connected to the plumbing system? Try them.

17.   Does the fireplace draw?

18.   Do all light switches and wall outlets work? Plug a small electric clock into each outlet to check it. Sheetrock crews frequently cover switches and outlets, causing an entire circuit to be inactive.

19.   Have you collected all instructions and warranties?

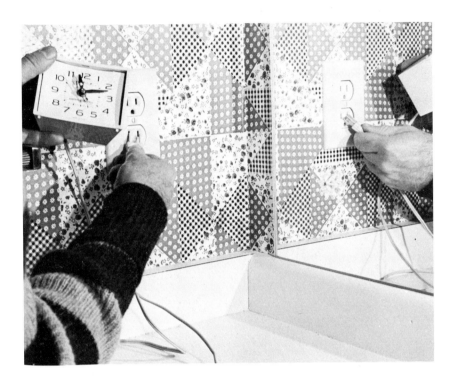

Plug an electric clock into every wall outlet. Some may never have been connected.

20. Whom should you call if something goes wrong? For how long do you have that privilege?

21. What can you expect as normal cracking, settling, and shrinking?

22. Has landscaping been done correctly for your climate?

23. Has the builder back-filled?

24. Will your yard drainage go into your neighbor's yard?

25. Where will your roof drainage go? Will it wash a gully in your yard?

26. Has all debris been hauled away?

27. Have you arranged for fire, hazard, and theft insurance to take up immediately when the builder's coverage stops?

28. Are all legal and financial matters in order?

29. Have you notified everyone of your change of address and erected your new mailbox?

30. Have you engaged the movers?

POSTSCRIPT

PEACE IN THE FAMILY

"You'll need money for a divorce too!" the banker said as he looked at us over the top of his glasses. A twinkle in his eye showed he was only jesting, but the meaning of his remark was quite clear. Our appointment with him was for a preliminary discussion of mortgage financing, and he, in his fatherly way, offered many other bits of sage advice as well. For 40 years he had dealt with home building in our area, and his opinions were well founded. He had watched many projects succeed and others fail, and he knew well what pitfalls lay ahead.

Tensions are to be expected because not only is a house the largest financial investment you may ever make, it is the materialization of your ideas. People are sensitive to criticism of their ideas, and this is the origin of most house arguments. You suddenly are faced with making decisions on insignificant little details you always took for granted, such as where to put the closet shelves. There will be as many answers as there are family members, and all but one will be displeased with the decision.

Children are unable to anticipate future pleasures in the new home as well as their parents can. They only know that something is completely consuming mama's and daddy's time, and their lovable parents have become ogres. Children may have undefined feelings of jealousy toward the house that appear as bad grades and misbehavior in school-age youngsters and reversions to infantile behavior in preschoolers. Thoughts of leaving old playmates and favorite neighborhood haunts to face the unknown new environment make children insecure. However, their real attitude is adopted from their parents, and genuine excitement and enthusiastic anticipation on the part of adults will transfer even to an infant and help to overcome childish fears and apprehensions. Little tots will feel they've made a contribution if they are allowed to hammer a nail or paint a board occasionally. Older children can help select finishing materials for their rooms, and they often have sound ideas to offer. *Involve all the children* as much as their ages and abilities allow so they will always look upon the house as "ours" rather than "yours."

Make special efforts to take a few minutes each day for "togetherness" with each child. It will help to keep the communication lines open and prevent jealousy and hatred of the house. The project can be a great learning experience also as the children watch the house grow right out of the ground, so explain to them what's going on and why. They will be proud to show off their new vocabulary and knowledge to their peers.

Mealtime, that once gracious repast, will be TV dinners and hamburgers when you begin in earnest because time once taken to meticulously prepare family favorites will be spent in building suppliers' showrooms, finance offices, and on the site waiting for workmen to show up. Many of your inspection trips can be turned into family picnics to be enjoyed leisurely after the workmen have left for the day. Keep the trips simple though; even a picnic can take hours of preparation if you insist on the old-fashioned kind. No banquet could ever equal the thrill of our first Christmas dinner at "Chinquapin." The menu was peanut butter and marmalade on slightly stale bread, with bought fruitcake for dessert, but we sat on the soft, sweet earth that had just been cleared the day before and visualized around us the dream that had begun to take shape.

Many frustrations can be avoided by planning your day's activities so the family can make a quick trip to the house after work. This may mean preparing supper in midafternoon to eat late after you return home, or putting it all in a basket and taking it with you. Many building supply firms close at noon on Saturday, so keep Saturday mornings free of other engagements to allow working members of the family a chance to see materials and help make selections.

Problems are much less troublesome to solve on paper in the planning stages than after building has begun. You will find that every moment you invest in careful thinking in the planning stage will yield great dividends in family harmony as well as in successful building.

MOVING

"We've got to be out by the first, and the house isn't finished yet. I don't know what we can do!" Our hysterical friend went on and on with her sad tale, one we've heard so many times we knew what was coming next. The people to whom our friends had sold their old house were ready to move in on the contract date, and the new house they had expected to be completed on that exact, same date wasn't ready.

It's nearly impossible to predict the day of completion for a new house with even the most competent builder because he is dependent on weather, labor, strikes, shortages, shipping, and a host of other factors in keeping the work moving at the necessary pace. Yet many people are so overwhelmed with the heady excitement of getting the project started that they blithely expect to move in on the completion date stated in the building contract and proceed to sign a sales contract on the old house promising to move out on that same date. In this way they get caught in a dilemma that causes them to exert pressure on their builder to rush the finishing details, that phase of building which above all others should not be rushed, while at the same time they must frantically find temporary quarters for their family. This is hardly the finale they pictured when they started. It involves both an unscheduled move and unscheduled expense because people under pressure grab the quickest thing available rather than bargain for something economical.

If you are presently living in a house you must sell, you can avoid this last-minute panic by *selling it before you start the new one*. Seek out an inexpensive apartment or rental house convenient to the building site and settle in for the duration of the building. The advantages of this plan are numerous. You are completely free of the old house to concentrate on the new one in the neutral, impersonal atmosphere of rented quarters. You no longer have to contend with showing the old one to a constant parade of prospective buyers who peer into innermost recesses of closets and cabinets and ask unnerving questions. If you sell first, your equity is completely free to be reinvested in the new house with all the bothersome paperwork of the sale behind you.

You can "camp" in the rental quarters, leaving everything packed and set aside except minimum necessities. This cuts down on housework and gives you an excellent opportunity to sort your belongings and discard or repair items not good enough for the new house.

Attention should be given to details of the rental lease to be sure you can leave on short notice without forfeiture of a large deposit, thus defeating part of your purpose in renting. Many rental agents are tolerant of such situations if you discuss them in the beginning, but *be certain*.

Long-distance moves across state lines and over federal highways are closely regulated by the Interstate Commerce Commission. It's difficult for a moving company to be dishonest on long-distance charges, but no such regulations govern local moves, and you must rely entirely on the integrity and ethics of the individual mover with whom you deal. Local charges usually are fixed on an hourly basis, making it easy for an unscrupulous driver to swell his profits with slow driving, long lunches, and by resetting his watch. Your best defenses against overcharges are to synchronize your watches and then follow the truck to your destination.

Moving day should be the most gratifying of all days because it's the final realization of a dream. Keep it free from frustrations, and enjoy every minute of it.

FORECASTERS OF DOOM

"Where's the guest room?" the uninvited visitor asked after she had completed her inspection of our new home. "There isn't one," we answered. She froze and was unable to conceal her shock and disapproval. "Oh, that's too bad, you'll be sorry you made that mistake. What will you do when your relatives want to visit?" she said. We smiled. . . .

Forecasters of doom—those kind and gentle friends, neighbors, and unknowns who are so anxious to point out all the mistakes you're making during construction and then offer predictions of future disasters that surely are inevitable. They just drop by to see how your new house is progressing—and add their bit of cheer. They come alone and in groups, and we don't know which is worse. Often they drop in when you are in the midst of conversation with the builder concerning tomorrow's work, or they arrive during the few minutes you and spouse are trying to make major decisions or solve emergencies. These bearers of glad tidings don't have ears—just mouths that are perpetually in motion. If you desperately try to explain the rationale behind your individual house, they never hear it. Their minds are set before they enter the site, and nothing you can say will ever change them. Of course, you have no obligation to justify anything you have chosen, but sometimes such people become unbearable and you feel like screaming, "Stop! It's *not* a mistake! This is the way we want it! *We're* going to live in it, not you." Don't waste your breath; the forecast will be made.

Not only must you expect the doom crew during every phase of construction, but for several weeks immediately after completion people will drop in "to see your new house." Some of these will be your close friends whom you will be happy to see, but occasionally near strangers will feel free to call (often immediately after breakfast) and inspect during this "open season." The remarks from them can be unbelievable. One lady left us speechless. After examining *everything* she made one comment, "I guess it'll be all right when it's decorated and furnished." It was already!

What is it about someone else's new home that transforms the nicest people into forecasters of doom? Perhaps psychologists can explain it, but understanding *why* they do it still won't help you remain civil when you are told that *your* desires, ideas, plans, and methods are all wrong, no good, and will result in failure and disappointment. Perhaps if you are aware of this psychological quirk, you can better insulate yourself against it. Comments will generally fall into these categories. These visitors will point out:

- All the bad things that will happen *during* the construction period

- All the bad things that will happen *after* the house is finished

- All the mistakes you have made that will make living in the house a miserable experience

These comments usually will be prefaced with, "I had a friend who did the same thing you are doing, and she was terribly unhappy with her house. It was just awful!" Notice she *had* a friend. The ex-friend probably is thrilled with her home, but the commentator has decided otherwise.

Some Words of Cheer and Encouragement That You May Hear

- "It won't be finished by that time. You'll probably have to move to a motel for a few months."

- "It'll never work."

- "How will you ever wash those windows? I wouldn't want that job!"

- "You'll never be able to heat it."

- "Your drive isn't wide enough. You could never manage a large truck in it."

- "Those trees are too close to the house. What if a tornado comes?"

- "I had a friend who used that kind of flooring. She said she loved it, but I know she didn't."

- "Your basement will smell. You'll probably have to put lime in it like we did."

- "Oh, I see you don't have a fireplace like mine. Well, you can't have everything at first. Maybe you can afford it later."

- "That kind of roof usually leaks, but maybe yours won't."

- "I guess it's okay, if this is the style you like."
- "It's interesting. . . ."

These words of cheer usually are based on the commentators' (1) personal failures and mistakes and (2) what they've imagined or heard that someone heard from someone else. Seldom are they based on fact.

How should you react? *Ignore them all.* What may be problems or undesirable features for them may be great for you. People expect everything to be like theirs, and when they are confronted with something different or unknown they often become defensive, and this is expressed in various ways. Should you ever listen to anyone? Yes. Listen to experienced experts who will gain nothing by offering comments, and by all means listen to your mortgage banker and take his advice!

"Carol built a house very much like this one and oh, what a terrible time she had. I don't want to discourage you, but the first thing that happened was. . . ."

AGENDA

		Chapters
1.	Select your lot.	2
2.	Engage an attorney.	2, 17, 21
3.	Plan your home to meet your needs.	3, 4, 5, 6, 7, 8, 9, 10, 11, 12, 13, 14, 15
4.	Discuss with lender approximate amount you can borrow (First Trip).	16
5.	Get preliminary plans.	17
6.	Select your builder.	18
7.	Revise the plans.	19, 20
8.	Make precautionary trip to lender (Second Trip).	16
9.	Have final plans drawn.	17
10.	Stop! Reevaluate.	20
11.	Have building contract drawn.	21
12.	Sign building contract.	21
13.	Apply for loan (Third Trip).	16
14.	Enjoy the building process.	22, 23, 24 Postscript
15.	Move.	Postscript

APPENDIX 1

ESTIMATE YOUR HOME-BUILDING POWER

WHAT CAN YOU SPEND MONTHLY FOR HOUSING?

1. **Your Average Monthly Income**
   Take-home pay* (gross pay less taxes) $_____
   Rents, dividends, interest†   _____
   Other Income   _____
       Net Average Monthly Income (add)   **(1)** $_____

2. **Your Average Monthly Non-Housing Expenses**
   Food, household supplies $_____
   Clothing   _____
   Medical costs and insurance   _____
   Life and casualty insurance   _____
   Automobile and insurance   _____
   Education   _____
   Commuting   _____
   Installment payments/interest charges   _____
   Recreation, hobbies (adjust realistically)   _____
   Telephone   _____
   Contributions, dues, fees, etc.   _____
   Personal (cleaning, barber, etc.)   _____
   Savings/investment program (adjust realistically)   _____
   Other miscellaneous expenses   _____
       Total Avg. Mo. Non-Housing Expenses (add)   **(2)** $_____

* You may include wages of a spouse who is working, or of other members of the family who live with you.

† Do not include dividends and interest from savings and investments you will use for down payment. Include only stable income sources.

3. Your Monthly Income Available for Housing

Net average Monthly Income (total 1) $_____

Subtract Non-Housing Expenses (total 2)   _____

Average Monthly Income Available for Housing Expenses   **(3)** $_____

4. Average Monthly Housing Expenses (of the home you wish to build)‡

Mortgage repayment (principal and interest) $_____

Comprehensive insurance for fire, theft, flood insurance (if not included in mortgage loan repayment)   _____

Property taxes (if not included in mortgage loan repayment)   _____

Utilities (heating, electricity/gas/oil, water)   _____

Maintenance and repairs (allow 1 percent or more of the price of your home *per year*)   _____

Other monthly housing expenses   _____

Average Monthly Housing Expenses (add) $_____

HOW MUCH DOWN PAYMENT CAN YOU AFFORD?§

5. Available Funds

Equity in present home/lot $_____

Savings, savings certificates   _____

Investments/mutual funds (current value)   _____

Insurance (cash surrender value)   _____

Other available funds (such as a personal loan)   _____

Total Available Funds (add) $_____

Subtract Amount you must keep in reserve   _____

Adjusted Total Available Funds   **(a)** $_____

6. Expected Cash Expenses

Cash costs for closing $_____

Furniture, furnishings (if any)   _____

Moving expenses   _____

Other expected expenses   _____

Total Expected Expenses (add)   **(b)** $_____

‡ Your builder and lender can probably approximate these costs for you. Now double-check your estimates. Check total 3 (what you can spend each month for housing) against total 4 (what you will need to spend each month for housing) to make sure that the home you are considering is within your means.

§ The money you have invested in your new lot also counts towards your down payment.

Now subtract total **(b)** (your expected expenses)
from total **(a)** (your available funds) to get
**amount you can afford to spend for your
down payment** **(c)** $_____

Note: Material in Appendix 1 is excerpted and adapted from NAHB Home Buyers
Guide by special permission of National Association of Home Builders. Copyright
NAHB.

APPENDIX 2

SUPPLIERS OF HOME PLANS

Action House Design Center
Residential Designer
548 E. Front Street
Traverse City, MI 49684

Architectural Graphics
Custom Home Designers, Stock
  Floor Plans, Planners
Sleepy Lagoon
Satellite Beach, FL 32935

Baton Rouge Plan Service
Planners, Architectural Draftsmen
9152 Mammoth Avenue
Baton Rouge, LA 70814

Better Homes and Gardens
Home Plan Dept. 6AC
1716 Locust Street
P.O. Box 374
Des Moines, IA 50336

L. M. Bruinier & Associates, Inc./
  Designers
1304 S.W. Bertha Blvd.
Portland, OR 97219

Buchan Plan & Design Service
Planners, Interior Designers
605 Whiting Avenue
Iowa City, IA 52240

Builders Design Service
Architects
Post Office Box 442
Edwardsville, IL 62025

Building Graphics, Inc.
Residential Planning & Design
1200 E. Morehead Street, #136
Charlotte, NC 28204

P. R. Chandler, Designer
1117 Lexington
Abilene, TX

Clinton Blueprinting
Architectural Draftsman & Designer
3191 Morse Road
Columbus, OH 43229

Collins, Harris & Key Designers
Building Designers
2340 N. Riverside Drive
Fort Worth, TX 76111

Complete Home Planning
Residential Designer
925 North Road
Fenton, MI 48430

Custom Design
House Designer
3000 W. Michigan Avenue
Lansing, MI 48917

Dalton Designs
Residential Design, Planners, Interior Designers
3618 N. 24th Street
Phoenix, AZ 85016

DB & Associates
Planners, Engineers
4411 Canyon Drive
Amarillo, TX 79110

Eden Plan Shop
Planners
1614 W. Randol Mill Road
Arlington, TX 76012

W. D. Farmer
Residence Designer, Inc.
P.O. Box 49463
Atlanta, Ga. 30359

Robert Fillmore and Associates
Designers–Plan Service
124 N.W. 67th Street
Oklahoma City, OK 73116

The Garlinghouse Company
320 S.W. 33rd Street
P.O. Box 299
Topeka, KS 66601

Gill & Son
Residential Designer
4747 Lee Street
Alexandria, LA 71301

James Grant Company, Inc.
Drafting
1710 Montgomery Highway
Dothan, AL 36301

Hamilton Design Service
Designer
1000 N. 38th Street
P.O. Box 153
Killeen, TX 76541

Tracy L. Hansen
Residential Designer
1641 Highland Avenue, E.
Twin Falls, ID 83301

Hardwicke Associates, Inc.
Planners, Interior Designers
6620 W. Broad Street
Richmond, VA 23230

Heritage Homes Plan Service, Inc.
Architects, Stock House Plans
550 Pharr Road, N.E., Suite 830
Atlanta, GA 30305

Hiawatha Estes
P.O. Box 404
Northridge, CA 91328

Home Builders Plan Service, Inc.
Home Designers
20 Marietta Street, N.W., Suite 1617
Atlanta, GA 30303

Home Building Plan Service
Professional Designers, Planners, Engineers
2235 N.E. Sandy Boulevard
Portland, OR 97232

Home Designers, Inc.
Architectural Design
1880 South Pierce Street
Lakewood, CO 80226

Home Planners, Inc.
Dept. BK
16310 Grand River Avenue
Detroit, MI 48227

Home Planning Service
Architectural Design, Planners
3125 Douglas Avenue
Des Moines, IA 50310

Homes for Better Living
P.O. Box 649
Forest Hills, NY 11375

House Beautiful
House-Plans Dept., Building
  Manual
P.O. Box 1701
Sandusky, OH 44870

House & Garden
Dept. BP-40
P.O. Box 1910
Grand Central Station
New York, NY 10017

Houston Design Group, Inc.
Residential Designers
1241 Blalock
Houston, TX 77055

KM Designs
Residential Designers, Planners
1174 E. 2700 So. Plaza #14
Salt Lake City, UT 84106

Thomas McCullough & Associates
Home Designers
108 Odette Street
Madison, TN 37115

Master Plan Service, Inc.
89 East Jericho Turnpike
Mineola, NY 11501

Modern Living Plan Service
Stock Plan Service
Box 608
Glen Ellyn, IL 60137

Red Moltz & Associates, Inc.
Residential Design, Planners
2082 Business Center Drive,
  #155
Irvine, CA 92715

Phillips & Company
Engineers, Planners
1016 Highway 90 Drive
Mobile, AL 36609

Piedmont Plan Service
Home Designers
201 Columbus Drive
Gaffney, SC 29340

Pitts Plan Services
Residential Designer, Planners,
  Light Commercial
4737 Saks Road
Anniston, AL 36201

Plan Service
Residential Drafting & Design,
  Planners, Architects, Interior
  Designers
3236 Garfield Street
Highland, IN 46322

Ray Prell & Associates, Inc.
Home Designers, Planners
12555 W. Burleigh Road
Brookfield, WI 53005

Ray's Plan Service
Residential Designers
2 F. Northwood Lake
Northport, AL 35476

R.C.K. Associates
Planners
455 Empire Boulevard
Rochester, NY 14609

Shelton Design & Blueprint
Residential Designers
1529 Jean Street
Montgomery, AL 36107

Stan Bailey Designer
Designer, Architectural Draftsman
2938 Hatcher Drive
Columbus, GA 31907

Studer Residential Designs
Residential Designers
412 Johns Hill Road
Cold Spring, KY 71076

Bobby N. Thompson & Associ-
ates
Residential Designers
Suite 230, 6350 LBJ Freeway
Dallas, TX 75240

Bill Trimble, Designer
Residential Designer
4900 North Protland, Suite 120
Oklahoma City, OK 73112

Don Van Eden, Residential
Drafting & Designing
Architects, Planners
1670 Ottawa Beach Road
Holland, MI 49423

INDEX